CRUNCH

WHY DO I FEEL SO SQUEEZED?
(AND OTHER UNSOLVED ECONOMIC MYSTERIES)

JARED BERNSTEIN

BK

Berrett–Koehler Publishers, Inc.
San Francisco
a BK Currents book

Berrett-Koehler Publishers, Inc.
235 Montgomery Street, Suite 650
San Francisco, CA 94104-2916
Tel: (415) 288-0260 Fax: (415) 362-2512   www.bkconnection.com

ORDERING INFORMATION

Quantity sales. Special discounts are available on quantity purchases by corporations, associations, and others. For details, contact the "Special Sales Department" at the Berrett-Koehler address above.

Individual sales. Berrett-Koehler publications are available through most bookstores. They can also be ordered direct from Berrett-Koehler:
Tel: (800) 929-2929; Fax: (802) 864-7626; www.bkconnection.com

Orders for college textbook/course adoption use. Please contact Berrett-Koehler:
Tel: (800) 929-2929; Fax: (802) 864-7626.

Orders by U.S. trade bookstores and wholesalers.
Please contact Ingram Publisher Services, Tel: (800) 509-4887; Fax: 838-1149;
E-mail: customer.service@ingrampublisherservices.com;
or visit www.ingrampublisherservices.com/Ordering for details about electronic ordering.

Berrett-Koehler and the BK logo are registered trademarks of Berrett-Koehler Publishers, Inc.

Printed in the United States of America

Berrett-Koehler books are printed on long-lasting acid-free paper. When it is available, we choose paper that has been manufactured by environmentally responsible processes. These may include using trees grown in sustainable forests, incorporating recycled paper, minimizing chlorine in bleaching, or recycling the energy produced at the paper mill.

LIBRARY OF CONGRESS CATALOGING-IN-PUBLICATION DATA

Bernstein, Jared.
    Crunch : why do I feel so squeezed? (and other unsolved economic mysteries) / by Jared Bernstein.
        p. cm.
    Includes bibliographical references.
    ISBN 978-1-57675-477-1 (hardcover : alk. paper)
    1. United States—Economic policy—2001- 2. Fiscal policy—United States.
    3. Cost and standard of living—United States. 4. Income distribution—United States.
    5. Globalization. I. Title.
    HC106.83.B472 2008
    330.973—dc22   2007046441

First Edition

13 12 11 10 09 08   10 9 8 7 6 5 4 3 2 1

Design and production by Seventeenth Street Studios
Copyediting by Elissa Rabellino and Kristi Hein
Index by Richard T. Evans

To my three children, Kate, Ellie, and Sarah.
May you gracefully meet all the challenges you face,
economic and otherwise.

Contents

Political Economy 202

The World Ain't Flat As All That

The Reconnection Agenda

Conclusion: The Lesson of the Rink   191

Preface

My name is Jared and I am a practicing economist.

I made my first graph decades ago, and while it sure felt good to see the way the bars lined up, I figured I could control the impulse. After a while, I was making several graphs and tables per hour, and talking earnestly about inflation, supply and demand curves, and Federal Reserve policy. I still thought I could stop whenever I wanted to.

It hasn't worked out that way. In fact, it's gotten much worse. I now go on TV shows and have raging arguments about tax cuts, trade balances, the minimum wage, and unemployment. Maybe you've seen me while flipping through the channels. Maybe you've wondered, whatever's got this guy so wound up?

I'll tell you. Economics has been hijacked by the rich and powerful, and it has been forged into a tool that is being used against the rest of us. Far too often, economists justify things many of us know to be wrong while claiming the things we believe are critically important can't be done.

I can't tell you how many times I've seen smart people with good hearts crumble in the face of economic arguments. Many of us will defer to such arguments, no matter how nuts these arguments seem, because they come shrouded in the mysterious authority of science. You might want to argue that unemployed people need a safety net when they lose their job, for example, but you're prone to back off the minute some economist points out how that will lead to "European levels of unemployment" or how it will "kill the person's incentive to find a job."

Maybe you've wondered whether all the tax cuts targeted at wealthy investors are really so necessary, especially given that we're spending borrowed money, only to be reminded that these tax cuts will spur investment and growth. Don't you get it? the story goes: We can't afford *not* to cut taxes!

At most, you might muster the gumption to say, "Well, I'm not an economist, but that doesn't sound right to me."

Well, I am an economist, and if I may ironically borrow a phrase from Ronald Reagan, I'm here to help.[1] It doesn't sound right to me either, and that's because it's wrong.

I'm tired of being stuck in the studio engaging in rants with Darth Vaders with PhDs. Wouldn't it be more useful to have an open-ended, rant-free dialogue with real, everyday people about their economic questions?

Maybe you've been wondering, is Social Security really going bust, and what does that mean to me? If I hire an immigrant, am I hurting a native-born worker? How much can presidents affect economic outcomes? What does GDP measure and what does it leave out? How come child care workers make so little? What does the "Fed" do, anyway? What's the cost of ignoring global warming? What's a "living wage"? And what *is* up with all those high-end tax cuts?

And of course, one that looms particularly large in the pages that follow: Why do I feel so squeezed?

In the following pages, I answer these and other questions. Though I sometimes tweaked them a bit, I did not make these questions up, nor did I poll my wonky economist friends. The questions come from non-economists, mostly taken from e-mail questionnaires and the blogosphere, where I've been having entirely too much fun "talking" about progressive economics and trolling for good questions.

What's a "good question"? Good question. I've got one main criterion. A good question, in the *crunchian* sense, is one that comes out of your everyday life as you interact with the economy, like the "Why do I feel so squeezed?" example above. Sometimes these quesitons grow out of people's run-ins with policy matters that leave them perplexed. The other night, for example, when my wife and I were burning far too many brain cells trying to figure out my employer's new health care plan, she started peppering me with questions about why our health care system is such a mess (jeez, you'd think a guy could catch a break at home . . .). A question might involve a moral dilemma, like the predicament of the woman who wondered if she should worry about the incentives involved in giving a dollar to a homeless person.

And lots of people wanted to learn what to make of key economic statistics, like gross domestic product and unemployment figures. What are they telling us? What's left out? For example, why, asked a perplexed but observant questioner, does the stock market often rise when the unemployment rate goes up? Seems counterintuitive, no?

Think of this book as a chance to hang out with someone who likes to tackle questions like these and promises to try to answer them in an engaging, non-jargony way. Come on, what do you say? How about it? Hey, where are you going? Get back here! Lemme show you this graph—I'm just getting started!

Introduction:
So What Is Economics, Anyway?

So a doctor tells this unfortunate woman that she has but six months to live. "Isn't there anything I can do?" she pleads. "Marry an economist," the doctor replies. "It won't cure the illness, but it will make the six months seem like five years."

We might as well start with the basics, and I promise this won't take anywhere near six months.

I recently completed my toughest speaking gig of the year: I taught an economics lesson to my first-grader's class. The goal was to teach them the fundamental concepts of needs versus wants, goods versus services, and scarcity. These distinctions are critical, because a good working definition of economics is the following:

> *The economy is the way we organize our society to best provide the goods and services*
> *that we need and want. Economics studies the best ways to do this.*

They quickly got the needs/wants distinction, but they raised some fascinating questions. They got that housing is a need. But someone then asked, "What about a mansion?" (Just to be sure, I asked them if they knew what a mansion was. "A big house with lots of cobwebs," they said.) They discussed that and determined that a mansion is a "want," not a need. Smart kids, I thought.

Anyway, all I'm saying is that anybody of any age can get this stuff. In fact, to not get it, to give up because it's too obscure, is, as I will show, a profoundly important political act, one with damaging consequences.

The stakes are high, for ourselves and for those who come after us—too high to entrust to those whose agenda is to redistribute power and resources to themselves and their friends.

Am I really suggesting that evil people disguised as social scientists are out to rob us blind while we willingly sign on the dotted line because we don't get the math?

No, not at all, though many powerful political and corporate actors use economists and economic (il)logic to do just that.

It's just that there are countless ways to organize our society to "best provide the goods and services that we need and want." In other advanced economies—in those of Europe, Canada, Scandinavia—they answer this question quite differently from the way we do. For example, they take access to health care services "out of the market," based on the beliefs (a) that health care is a basic right in an advanced society, and (b) as discussed in some detail later, that there are special attributes of health care that make unregulated markets a particularly inefficient (read: wasteful) way to deliver and provide it. And you don't have to get on a plane to learn the lesson that there are different ways to organize the economy. In other periods within our own history, we organized things differently, too.

This question of how we organize the economy matters a lot. It determines how the benefits of growth are distributed. Even more important, it determines who gets the opportunity to realize their potential. If the best educational opportunities go to the haves, their position relative to the have-nots will become etched in stone, as economic mobility atrophies. If those in political power believe—and act on the belief—that labor standards, like minimum wages, overtime, or the right to collectively bargain, are harmful to economic growth, then the ability of some workers to bargain for their fair share of the growing economy will evaporate while that of others grows stronger. How we organize our economy determines how we structure our response to the challenges from environmental degradation, globalization, the lack of health coverage, and staggering wealth inequalities.

When answering the questions that follow, three unifying principles kept coming up. I'll come back to these often, as I found them to be useful navigational tools, providing the intellectual and moral guideposts needed to keep us moving in the right direction—toward an economy that works best for all.

BASIC PRINCIPLES OF CRUNCH-STYLE ECONOMICS

1. Economic outcomes are generally thought to be fair, in the sense that market forces dole out rewards to those who merit them. But that's not always the case. Power, whether it's based on political clout, wealth, class, race, or gender, is also a key determinant of who gets what.

2. Economic relationships often play out in surprising ways, contradicting both basic logic and textbook theory. The path to economic truth is paved with evidence, not assumptions.

3. Since economics is concerned with finite resources, economic decisions often invoke trade-offs: choosing one outcome over another. Though these trade-offs are usually thought of as the benign outcomes of rational discourse, it's not so: See #1.

As I hope these principles suggest to you, the goal of this book is not simply to help readers become better versed in economic discourse, though that's part of my goal. It's also to offer a new way to answer the question, how can we best organize our society to provide the things we want and need? America is a democracy, and in a democracy we all get to weigh in on biggies like this, not just the elites and their scholarly shock troops.

With that in mind, let's get to work.

Crunchpoint:* Economics is not an objective, scientific discipline. It is a set of decisions about how to produce and distribute resources and opportunities. Understanding

---

* Each question and chapter in the book ends with a "crunchpoint," an allegedly snappy summary of the discussion.

and evaluating the logic and rationales for those decisions, while recognizing whom those decisions favor or exclude, is a big part of what this book is about. To proceed with these insights foremost in our minds is the only way I know to rechannel the power of economic analysis back to the service of those who need it most: the ones in the vise grip of the crunch.

1

The Big Squeeze

Why do I feel so squeezed?

As I solicited questions for this book, the one above kept coming up, in one form or another. And while I'm not happy about that, it is affirming, because it is, in my view, the great, unanswered economics question of our time.

It's not that middle-class people are sliding into poverty, hunger, and homelessness, though in an economy as wealthy as ours, too many people do face those conditions. The sense I got from questioners, a sense I've tried to convey in the answers I offer below, is that something is "off" in the new economy. We hear great economic news about financial markets, prices, profits, growth, productivity, and globalization, yet many of us live with a weight of economic anxiety that our parents would not have recognized. Most of us are making progress as we age, but the path seems steeper than we might have expected, with deeper potholes along the way. For some of us, things we aspire to, like secure health care or the ability to send our kids to a good college without taking on a lot of debt, are still within our grasp, but we have to reach farther to grab them, and it's harder to hold on.

For others of us, a bit farther down the income scale, these aspirations are fading. To our surprise, we find ourselves without health coverage, or unable to afford the premiums and co-payments. We're stuck in a house and a neighborhood we thought we'd have grown out of by now, with a school to which we'd rather not send our kids. And while we're working as hard as ever, that paycheck is alarmingly thin after gas and groceries.

Not everyone feels that way. Raise the issue of the squeeze, and many economists and policymakers will excitedly (and correctly) remind you productivity is soaring! . . . unemployment's historically low! . . . inflation's down!

How do I know this? Because I'm a regular on CNBC's *Kudlow & Company*, a show that focuses largely on stock and bond markets. It's almost infectious, the way Larry Kudlow and his guests from the world of financial markets bubble over with effusive, heartfelt praise for all those positive trends just mentioned. To them, for example, globalization means a greater supply of capital and labor, "more global liquidity," lower prices, lower interest rates, and a lot more people with whom to make trades. To millions of others, globalization means greater wage competition and less job security. They're both right.

I'm fortunate that these financial market mavens will at least entertain a different perspective, but no matter how many times I point out that the typical working family's purchasing power—its inflation-adjusted income—is actually down over their beloved economic boom, they can't hear me.

Why not? Well, like they say, denial ain't just a river in Egypt. It's a place to which lots of economic elites retreat so that they can avoid the tough question, what's behind the divergence between the macroeconomy and the microeconomy, between stock portfolios and paychecks, between the view from Wall Street and the view from Main Street?

Let us begin by presenting some evidence, and then tackle that critical question.

The statistics behind the squeeze are embarrassingly easy to come by. Anybody with a mouse can stop puzzling over this after a precious few clicks.

■ The economy grew by 15 percent between 2000 and 2006, but the inflation-adjusted weekly earnings of the typical, or median, worker were flat (down 0.7 percent; the *median* is the worker at the 50th percentile, right in the middle of the wage scale).[1]

- Partly due to the jobless recovery that lasted until mid-2003 (I discuss recessions and recoveries later on), the typical working-age household's income was down 5 percent, or $2,400, from 2000 to 2006.[2] Their income was down more than their wage because they found fewer available hours of work.

- After falling steeply in the latter 1990s, the share of the population that's officially poor rose from 11.3 percent in 2000 to 12.3 percent in 2006, the most recent available data point for poverty rates.[3]

- While inflation overall has been moderate since 2000, as I point out below, the costs of some of the key components of the middle-income market basket—health care, child care, college tuition, housing—have been growing much faster than the overall average of all prices taken together.[4]

That's a lot of numbers, but let's not gloss over them. Over the course of this highly touted economic expansion, poverty is up, working families' real incomes are down, and some key prices are growing a lot faster than the average.

Now, I know you don't hear about such numbers every day—instead, you hear about the stock market every hour. But these statistics are not secret.

It's obviously important to document the facts, but it's also useful to look beyond the statistics to people's own views about the economy. Such views jump around to some extent with highly visible indicators like gas or home prices, but in one weekly poll (ABC–*Washington Post*), more than half of respondents have registered negative impressions about the economy since the summer of 2001. Clearly, dissatisfaction with the Iraq War dominated the 2006 midterm elections, but the economy was next in line. According to the *New York Times* exit poll, two-thirds of voters in November 2006 reported that they were either just maintaining their living standards (51 percent) or falling behind (17 percent). By 2007, 44 percent said they lacked the money they needed "to make ends meet," up from 35 percent a few years earlier.[5]

Remember—this is a critical part of the story—the cheerleaders are right, in their own narrow way. While all these unsettling poll results were coming in, the economy was expanding at a good clip and generating stellar rates of productivity growth.[6] We were achieving efficiency gains at a rate that hadn't been seen in over 30 years. The unemployment rate was low in 2006–07, below 5 percent. The stock market took a dive in late 2000, but by the end of 2006 it was up 56 percent from its '03 trough. Five years into this recovery, corporate profits as a share of national income were at a 56-year high and were percolating along at a rate more than twice the average of past recoveries. Yet more than 4 in 10 told pollsters they were having trouble making ends meet.

What this barrage of percentages is telling us is that if you feel squeezed, chances are it's because you *are* squeezed. Most of the indicators that matter most to us in our everyday lives—jobs, wages, mid-level incomes, prices at the pump and the grocery store, health care, retirement security, college tuition—are coming in at stress-inducing levels, but gross domestic product (GDP), our broadest measure of the economy's health, explained later, keeps on truckin'.

Something's wrong, something fundamental. Not Third World–poverty fundamental, not blood in the streets, massive homelessness, or Great Depression fundamental. If the problem were that obvious, it would be less amorphous, less indecipherable, less of a head-scratcher.

The name of the problem is *economic inequality*, and it's been on the rise for decades. It's at the heart of the squeeze, and it's a sign that something important is broken: the set of economic mechanisms and forces that used to broadly and fairly distribute the benefits of growth. What "mechanisms" am I thinking of? They are unions, minimum wages, employer and firm loyalty, global competitiveness, full employment, the robust creation of quality jobs, safety nets, and social insurance, all of which are discussed in the following pages.

The belief that growth should be fairly distributed, that the bakers should get their slice, is a fundamental economic value in America. It is, of course, not one we have always lived up to, especially for the least advantaged among us. But it's always there, this sense that the rising tide should lift the rowboats and the houseboats, not just the yachts. When the lesser boats founder, people know it. And that's where we are today. Bill Clinton won an election appealing to those people in 1992, various senators and congresspeople did so in 2006, and, from what you could hear as the 2008 campaign season got under way (much too early for the taste of most of us), the Democratic presidential candidates were tapping directly into the same set of values.

Now, you won't hear this description of our economic challenges from most op-ed writers, any presidents, or central bankers. Their answer to the inequality question comes down to one, and only one, solution: more education. They believe that the reason the economy is passing so many folks by is that they don't have the smarts and skills to cash in on the opportunities we're creating.

The education mantra is a clever framing because (a) it rings true— you're always better off with more education, and (b) it subtly puts the burden on you. The message is, "The opportunities to get on the right side of the inequality tide are there, if you're smart enough." If you're not, well, then, either smarten up and join the parade or stop whining. As one U.S. Treasury official put it, "If the country . . . is going to undergo economic growth, then the population has to be able to take advantage of opportunities."[7] Or, as President George W. Bush elliptically put it, "We have an economy that increasingly rewards education and skills because of that education."[8]

Ten years ago, he would have been at least partly right. Today, education is neither the main cause of nor the main solution to the inequalities we face.

I deal with this in greater detail in a later chapter, but for now, I'll assert that inequality is no longer being driven by the highly skilled pulling away from the rest of the pack. Yes, you're far better off with a college education than without, but that degree won't insulate you from global competition. Especially if your work can be digitized and offshored, there are highly skilled but low-paid workers in other countries with whom you now compete. The real wages of American college grads rose less than 2 percent from 2000 to 2006.

Yet, while college grads are beginning to feel the same competitive pinch that the blue-collar workers have felt for years, the share of income going to the top 1 percent of households in 2005 was, at 22 percent, higher than in any year since 1929!

Therefore, a simple "big skills get big rewards" story just doesn't cut it today. To understand what's behind today's inequality, something to which I devote considerable time in the coming pages, you've got to deal with principle #1: POWER. More so than in any recent period, those who hold a privileged position in the economic power hierarchy, the players who sit down at the poker table with a stack of chips reaching to the ceiling—the CEOs and the holders of large capital assets—are able to steer the bulk of growth their way. Then, using their political connections, they're able to ice the cake with a nice bit of after-tax redistribution, as regressive changes in the tax code funnel even more resources their way.

The rest of us—those who sit down with a modest stack of chips—are left trying to figure out . . . well, like it says in the title, why do I feel so squeezed?

Crunchpoint: You feel squeezed because you are squeezed. If this were just a growth problem, we could have a nice, polite discussion of ways to get productivity humming again, or how to bring down the unemployment rate. But productivity's been great and unemployment's low. The squeeze is on, and we won't be able to call it off until we deal with our inequality problem.

Before wading more deeply into the etiology of the crunch, how about a nice mystery story?

I've always enjoyed the noir style in films and books, where gritty gumshoes pursue mysterious ladies while snarled in deeply tangled plots. One evening, while struggling to reconcile the growing economy with falling wages, I felt unusually close to Humphrey Bogart and wrote this story. In the next chapter, I explain the concept of gross domestic product in greater depth. But it's simply our broadest measure of economy-wide growth. I also mention Ben Bernanke, chairman of the Federal Reserve, in the story.

I was working late in my DC office. I'd been running some new simulations on my macro-model, but nothing was converging, so I figured I'd close up my spreadsheet and find a corner in some dark speakeasy to lick my wounds.

That's when she walked in. She had a neckline as low as the Nasdaq in '01, curves like sine waves, and a dress tighter than the global oil supply. She had my attention even before she pulled out two reports I'd seen that very morning.

"I'm sorry to barge in on you like this," she said in a voice that gave my calculator a power surge. "I didn't know where else to turn."

"You came to the right place, doll," I said. "I see you've got the first-quarter GDP report, along with the new compensation results." I'd been puzzling over these numbers all day, but what, I wondered, could this tall glass of cool water want with them?

"That's right," she purred. "I need to know why GDP is up 4.8 percent, the strongest quarter since 2003, yet real wages are falling." Yeah, I thought, you and everybody else who works for a living.

"Why the interest?" I shot back. She didn't look like a Democrat.

"I wish I could tell you. But I work for some powerful people"—now I knew she wasn't a Democrat—"and they'd be very upset if they knew I was here."

"Why me? Why don't you ask your powerful friends to explain why the economy's racing ahead but leaving working stiffs behind?"

She got kinda sulky, and I kinda liked it. "They wouldn't know where to look. What's worse, most of them think it's great when wage growth decelerates because with no inflationary pressure from labor costs, it means the Fed can take a powder on rate increases."

"Tell me about it, sister. I've been leaning on Bernanke for months on that point, but he doesn't return my calls."

Needless to say, I took the case. I wasn't sure what game Little Miss Conflicting Reports was playing, but I figured I'd play along for now.

Fact is, I'd been asking the same question myself. Every quarter we seemed to be getting great news on top-line statistics—GDP, productivity, profits—yet the typical worker's real earnings were down 2 percent over the recovery. Guys like me don't like it when things line up that way.

I headed for the union hall, figuring some of those people might have an angle. Problem was, with private-sector unions down to 8 percent of the workforce, the hall had become a Starbucks. I got a vanilla chai latte to go and beat it.

I decided to head for the new economy, so I looked up some managers and professionals in the service sector. I found them, all right, but they didn't have any answers. As of the first quarter of 2006, their compensation had lagged inflation for three quarters running.

This was more serious than I'd thought. Whatever was driving a wedge between overall growth and living standards, it was reaching pretty high up the pay scale. I wasn't sure what mess I'd gotten into here, but it was time to confront the doll that got me into it.

I caught up with her in her penthouse, a place that had "housing bubble" written all over it. I know my wealth distributions, and this kitten came from the top 0.1 percent. I don't like playing the sap—it was time for some class warfare.

"OK, gorgeous. Drop the 'two Americas' line and give it to me straight. You know as well as I do where the growth is going. What's your game?"

She nibbled her lip and looked up at me real sweet. "I suppose if I told you I'm just a girl who cares about the bottom 99 percent, you wouldn't believe me."

She supposed right.

"All right, I'll come clean," she said, slumping in a chaise longue that probably cost the average income of the bottom fifth. "I work for the Republican National Committee, and we're starting to get spooked by the president's poll numbers on the economy. We figured if we don't get a little trickle-down soon, it could hurt us in 2006, not to mention '08."

I kicked myself for not seeing it sooner. "So you don't give a damn about the structural factors driving the productivity/wage gap: the declining unions, low minimum wage, the profit squeeze, slack job creation, and most of all the way globalization is sapping the bargaining clout of the American worker, blue and white collar alike."

"Why should I?" she said, finally showing her true colors. "Any intervention would just cuff the invisible hand, doing more harm than good." She was Milton Friedman with the body of Scarlett Johansson. I had to get outta there.

"You're wrong!" I shouted, staggering toward the door. "You can't see it, but these two reports are a microcosm of everything that's right and wrong with this economy. Tell your people that whoever understands and articulates this disconnect, along with offering a convincing policy agenda to reconnect growth and living standards—that's who wins the big tamale."

I was wasting my breath. She had me bounced by a security guard as pumped up as ExxonMobil's profits.

I brushed the dust off my suit and headed for the office. You'd think a case like this would be dispiriting to a guy like me, but you'd be wrong. Sure, she'd made me mad, but I saw things clearly now, and her little scheme was about to backfire.

There's an electorate out there that's looking for some economic stewardship. Maybe I'm just one economist in this big, crazy city, and maybe the other guys've got the deep pockets. But the way I see it, we can shape our economic outcomes so that everyone gets a fair shake, not just the chosen few.

I opened up a spreadsheet and got to work.

OK, that squeeze stuff is pretty convincing. But I hear a lot of cheerleaders touting a different set of facts, and once economists start throwing these numbers around, I'm lost. How can I tell if presidents/politicians/economists are giving it to me straight? What's the right scorecard?

That's a great and critical question, one that reminds me of my days teaching statistics. On day one of the course, we'd have a wide-ranging discussion about the use of statistics in society, and someone always— and I mean without exception—raised the argument that statistics was a fancy way to make stuff up. I lay in wait for this argument, and my response was that, in fact, the point of learning this stuff was to be able to distinguish between bad and good statistics.

My sense at the time was that my explanation probably convinced only a precious few, but the idea is an important one for our journey through *Crunchland*. Folks on cable news shows aren't the only ones who selectively pick which facts they want to feature about the economy. Presidents do, too, and that creates a lot of cognitive dissonance among those stuck in the crunch. Here's a scorecard to help square the difference between what you hear and what you see.

Like the rooster who's sure his crowing caused the sunrise, presidents, regardless of party—this is not, I repeat not, a partisan critique (though I am fully capable of such critiques, and you'll bump into more than a few along the way)—will always take credit for anything good that happens in the economy. And they're not above picking the cherry tree clean to do so.

To do so, they generally use three methods: strategic clock starting, broad averages, and bars so low that even they can get over them.

A posting on the White House Web site ("Hey, didn't you just say something about this not being a partisan attack?" . . . Yes, but I'm picking on Bush here because, since he's the prez, his spin is a mouse-click away, and, truth be told, his folks engage in this stuff more than most), accessed in November 2007, for example, makes the following claims:[9]

More than 8.31 million jobs created since August 2003.

Granted, you may annoy anyone within hearing distance, but when economists start spouting numbers, remember this invaluable question: "Compared to what?"

"More than 8.31 million" sounds big, right? But in a workforce of 150 million, it's a rate of job growth that's actually well behind the historical average. It also comes after years of employment losses, even as the economy expanded—another example of the disconnect we face today.[10]

Since economic data series tend to fluctuate with the business cycle, trending negative in recessions and improving over recoveries, you can make any data series sing whatever tune you want if you start counting at a carefully chosen point in time. When looking at longer-term trends, economists avoid this bias by comparing similar points in the business cycle, the most common being peak-to-peak.

It's analogous to when you weigh yourself. If you wanted to convince yourself you were losing weight, you'd take your baseline weight right after a big meal, then check your progress first thing in the morning (hey, I'm going to try that!).

In this case, the Bush-league econ wizards, recognizing that their boy had presided over the worse jobless recovery on record (though the recession was over in November 2001, we kept losing jobs until August 2003), started the clock in August 2003. If they'd done it the right way, they'd have to report that job growth over the Bush cycle has been the worst on record, going back to the 1940s.

Real wages rose 1.2 percent over the past 12 months.

Ah, the soft bigotry of low expectations. One percent real growth isn't nothin', but it's way too close for comfort.

And anyway, compared to what? (See, you can start using that one right away.) Real wages were no higher when the White House made this announcement than they were three years earlier (real wages fell from 2004 through the first half of 2006).[11] And over the longer term, wage growth for different groups of workers should always be compared with productivity, answering the question, are the bakers getting a fair slice of the pie?

Over the business cycle from 2001 to 2007, real wages were up 2.3 percent, compared with 18 percent for productivity, a sure sign that slices were not growing in proportion to the pie. That's a gain of about $0.40 per hour (the average wage was $17.24 in April 2007), or around $800 for a full-year worker over six years: $133 per year. If your benchmark for success is essentially zero, then you'll pop the champagne cork for even the most marginal gain.

Again, that's what presidents do, and not just this president. Back in Bill Clinton's first term, my organization published a critical review of the administration's claims about the quality of jobs "they'd created"— that is, created on their watch. They pointed out that lots of the new jobs were in higher-paying occupations. We showed that (a) this is almost always the case—occupation upgrading is the norm (note the use of the classic compared-to-what technique), and (b) many of these supposedly good jobs were paying less than they used to. (Note: Back then, we got invited over to the White House for a nice lunch, wherein we spoke earnestly about our competing analyses; I waited and waited to hear from the Bushies, but my wait was in vain.)

Real after-tax income per person has risen by 12.7 percent, more than $3,800 per person, since the president took office.

Another classic tactic: Cite broad averages, ignoring the fact that the benefits of growth have been anything but broadly shared. Exacerbate the crime by implying that they have ("$3,800 per person").

Imagine an economy with five people, each of whom earns, respectively, 1, 2, 3, 4, 5 bucks. The average and the median are both 3. Now, imagine that the income of the top person jumps to $100. The average is now 22 (4 bucks more per person![12]), but the median is still 3. In other words, the median is insensitive to big jumps at the top.

Unfortunately, this is no thought experiment. It's representative of the growth concentration that occurred through the first half of the 2000s.[13]

Crunchpoint: In the interest of statistical inoculation, invoke these simple rules when presidents and sundry economic types start throwing numbers around:

- Ask "Compared to what?" Most economic variables grow most of the time, so the question is not whether X (employment, incomes, wealth, and so on) is growing, but by how much relative to what we'd expect in normal times. Don't be moved by large numbers with no historical context.

- Broad averages, such as income per person, are distorted by the huge values of the richest households, so remember this handy rhyme:

When it's inequality you're seein',
Don't use the average, use the median.

My dad had a full-time job, but my mom didn't, and they managed to raise, feed, house, and educate two kids on one salary. I can't do that today. Why not? What happened?

What happened was that the real earnings of lots of people, mostly male people, so husbands in this case, started to slip. At the same time, some of the very costs mentioned—a home and a college education—grew a lot faster than average inflation (and the fact that this questioner is from San Francisco makes a difference here, especially regarding home prices).

That's bad.

Also, over the last 30 years, the job market has opened up much more for women, who have made impressive gains that have helped to offset their husbands' wage stagnation.

That's good.

But it also means that family members are spending a lot more time in the job market. That's bad, or at least it's stressful.

There are three problems here and one positive development.

Problem 1: Men's earnings.

The hourly earnings of some men—and not a trivially small group—have done poorly over the last few decades. As shown in the graph, the typical married man in his prime earning years, age 25 to 54, saw his real median wage fall a couple of percent from 1979 to 2006. His female counterpart made a lot more progress; her real hourly wage rose 30 percent, and she also worked a lot more hours. And if we cut the data a little further and look at husbands with at most a high school degree—and only a minority of husbands were college educated over these years (16 percent in the mid-1970s; 30 percent today)—we find a real wage loss of 8 percent over these 27 years.

But before you spouses out there start humming "Hit the road, Jack," recognize that it's not their fault. These men have been caught in the

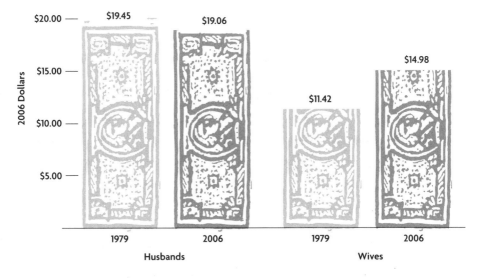

Figure 1.1. Real median hourly wage, husbands and wives, 1979–2006.
(Graph is based on author's analysis of U.S. Census Bureau data.)

crossfire of a set of trends that have ripped the bottom out of their earnings capacity. The loss of unionized factory jobs has meant the slow bleed of high-productivity jobs in a sector where these guys had some bargaining power—clout that enabled them to channel some of that growth into the household.

The fact is, when a man goes from making stuff to providing services, especially a man without a college degree, his wage falls between 15 and 20 percent, and he loses most of his fringes.[14] What explains a loss of that magnitude? It's not just the difference in the efficiencies between the two sectors, the so-called productivity differential—the fact that services create less value added per hour than factory work. It's also that there's a lot more wage inequality in services, and when income grows in that sector, it tends to flow to the top.

That's where you most clearly see men's loss of bargaining power playing out; and outside of the public sector, unions have been hard-pressed to get a foothold in services. Wal-Mart has shut down operations rather than entertain the possibility of their workers forming a union.

At any rate, given that most of these men were working full time, full year, families had one (legal) strategy to undertake if they wanted to off-set those negative male wage trends: more work by wives.

Problem 2 and Good Development 1: Women's increased presence in the paid labor market.

The increase in women's participation in the paid labor market over the last 40 years is widely appreciated as a huge change in our economy, our culture, and our families. Back in the mid-1960s, about 40 percent of women worked; in 2006, it was about 60 percent. And, while gender wage discrimination was and is a problem, women have made important gains in education and experience, and some have successfully penetrated barriers in high-end professions like law and medicine.[15]

The wage differences noted above are dramatic, and working wives, for example, have more than offset husbands' losses. My own research has shown that in the absence of wives' added contributions to family income, the real (inflation-adjusted) income of middle-income married-couple families with kids would have gone up a mere 6 percent between 1979 and 2000, a barely noticeable advance of 0.3 percent per year.[16]

Instead, it was up 25 percent (1 percent per year). That's the difference between stagnation and rising living standards. My guess is that families like that of the man who asked this question looked at the lay of this land and recognized that if they wanted a better life for their children, they were going to need to spend more time in the paid-job market. The men were topped out, already working full time, full year. And the upside is that working women were both taking advantage of increased economic opportunities and building some important economic independence.

But consider this. Husbands in these families were already working full time, and that hasn't changed much at all. Wives, on the other hand, are working more weeks per year and more hours per week. In fact, they worked, on average, 535 more hours in 1979 than they did in 2000, the equivalent of more than three months of full-time work (they went from about 850 hours per year to about 1,390).

That's one source of the squeeze that working families are talking about these days. You could write a book about that too, but let me summarize very simply: It's a bitch to balance work and family when you and the spouse are working one and three-quarters full-time, full-year jobs between you. It can be done, families do it every day, and we should never downplay the empowerment endowed by greater economic independence. But it's exhausting.

Problem 3: Faster price growth for some important stuff.

When people talk about the middle-class squeeze, what they're really saying is that their paycheck isn't going as far as it used to. Now, economists (like me) who look at overall inflation and compare that with incomes often miss what's at the heart of these concerns, and at the heart of the question we're parsing through: Your income can be beating overall inflation but falling behind on some highly visible and very important areas of your budget, your life, and your perfectly reasonable aspirations.

Over the past decade—1996 to 2006—overall prices as measured by the Consumer Price Index were up about 30 percent, a pretty typical rate of price growth. But the costs of child care and nursery school rose twice as fast—they were up 60 percent. College tuition: up 80 percent. The price of the median home doubled over those years, from $110,000 to $220,000 (of course, there was a bubble at work here—see Chapter 2). Health premiums—the monthly amount that families pay out of pocket for employer-provided coverage—also just about doubled, from $122 to $226.

Obviously, if these goods and services are outpacing overall inflation by a country mile, other goods are diving in price. And yes, if you've shopped for a DVD or computer lately, you know what I'm talking about. Later, in the section on globalization in Chapter 4, I describe my adventure when I went shopping for a music system. The price of audio equipment is down 40 percent over the last decade. Computer prices are down 86 percent![17]

Here we have the other answer to Bob's "What happened?" While economists blissfully celebrate the price declines of cool shiny new stuff with keyboards and remote controls, some of those clunky old things that kind of get us through life, the stuff for which we write checks each month—mortgages, health insurance premiums, child care, the kids' college-saving account (if we're lucky)—have been costing a lot more, and, even for many upper-income families, their prices have been rising more quickly than incomes. Don't get me wrong: It's great to be able to buy an awesome computer or sound system for pocket change. They're very entertaining after an exhausting day of being squeezed by everything else.

Crunchpoint: The fact that lots of men have been whacked by globalization, deunionization, and deindustrialization shows up as real wage trends that have barely kept pace with inflation. Women, on the other hand, have done better in terms of wage growth, and they're spending much more time in the job market. For many families, that's more than offset the husband's wage losses, but it comes at a cost: Balancing work and family is much harder now. Add the fact that the prices of some key components of the middle-class budget are rising faster than middle-class incomes, and you've got the genesis of the "middle-class squeeze." And that's why the family of the man who asked this question can't live like his parents' family did.

Haiku-nomics: Sure, we can talk about economics all day. But at some point, you want to hear some poetry, right? In that spirit, you will be introduced to a new form of Zen-based poetry I call haiku-nomics, strategically placed throughout the book. The haiku is a simple Japanese form intended to plant an image, idea, or fleeting feeling in the mind of the listener. Now, there may be a reason why the great haiku artists of the distant past avoided economic themes. You be the judge.

■ **The economy grows.
Yet my resources fail
to reach my needs.**

Health care reformers, from Michael Moore to scholarly wonks, constantly tell us that some other countries spend less on health care, cover more people, and have better health care outcomes than we do. Is it so, and if it is, are we going to do something about it?

One of the most important aspects of the middle-class squeeze relates to people's concerns around health care, a topic about which many folks raise questions. Other countries spend less on health care because they recognize it is not something that can be efficiently produced and delivered through a purely market system. So they take it at least partially out of the market; that is, the government sector plays a much larger role in both access to and delivery of health care. In doing so, these other countries undermine the damaging power and scope of the medical industrial complex—the MdIC—a force that must be met if we're ever going to get this right. Principle #1 comes first for a reason: Our biggest economic reform challenges, and I'd put health care at the top of that list, have been and will continue to be a struggle to wrest power from those with deeply vested interests in maintaining their privileged positions.

The advantage that reformers have in this debate is that there are demonstrable ways—systems up and running in other advanced economies—to provide health care more efficiently and effectively than we do now. Getting there will be neither easy nor painless nor devoid of sacrifice. But as I document later, unless we change course, health care spending will simply suck up too many of our resources, leaving too little for anything else.

Just for the record, this is not a radical claim, nor is it something unknown to most economists. Congress's nonpartisan budget analyst, the Congressional Budget Office, regularly churns out documents pointing out . . . well, not so much that "the end is near," but more, "You guys are going to want to do something about the ever-increasing share of health care in our economy . . . right, guys? Hello? Anyone there?"

Given these economic pressures, let me first dispose of the easier second question: I think and hope that we may be poised to at least start moving in the right direction on health care. Granted, that's not a hugely confident assertion, but let's face it: When it comes to making big changes in big, important systems, we don't exactly turn on a dime. But let's also face this fact: People get that the current system is breaking down, and politicians seem to get that people get it. A poll from early 2007 found that a majority wanted Congress to address the problem of health care coverage and 60 percent were even willing to pay higher taxes to deal with it. Almost 8 out of 10 said it was more important to make sure that people got health care than to extend the Bush tax cuts.[18]

It's no surprise that people want better health care, but when they start saying they're ready to pay higher taxes, that should get everyone's attention. These days, it seems every serious political candidate has a plan purporting to deal with health insurance, often highlighted as the centerpiece of his or her campaign.[19] All this attention won't guarantee a desirable outcome (we'll talk about competing health plans in Chapter 5), but it does tell you that the issue is solidly on the front burner. As I stress below, there are powerful forces aligned against health care reform, and my guess is that we'll move toward the light (that is, a better system) in baby steps.

About the first part of the question: As noted, every other advanced economy has recognized that health care coverage is not a commodity like picnic tables or pet food, and so, to one degree or another, either they provide it through the public sector or, if they keep it private, it's highly regulated. This might sound odd to free market advocates, whose religion holds that any service taken out of the market or highly regulated will be provided less, not more, efficiently.

But health care is different from commodities in some fundamental ways. First, since we tend not to let people expire in the streets, we end up providing the uninsured with care. If a hungry person shows up at a supermarket without money, he doesn't get fed. But if a sick person shows up at the hospital without insurance, she does get treatment. And the rest of us end up paying for it.

Another reason why we shouldn't be thinking of health care as a commodity is that it's one of those things that sellers—the insurers—want to sell less of, especially to sick people. Private insurers have an incentive to prevent people from getting all the care they think they need. This incentive rises as medical costs rise, and health costs have been rising a lot faster than average inflation. Remember, insurers are in the for-profit sector, and while of course they expect to make all kinds of payouts to the people they cover, they're going to spend some time and resources trying to avoid doing so. Basically, the sicker you are, the more you need access to the system. But you are precisely the person the gatekeepers want to keep out. It's a recipe for dysfunction.

Other countries with advanced economies save a lot by taking the insurers out of the picture. As noted, they employ either *single-payer* or heavily regulated systems, in which either the government is the exclusive insurer or private insurers must provide specified, subsidized coverage to all.[20] There's little market competition, but costs are held down by (1) taking advantage of the huge risk pool—when the nation has one insurer to which you have to contribute, the majority of healthy people subsidize the minority of sick people; (2) the absence of profits, advertising, and weeding-out costs (it takes insurers time and resources to get between people and the care they want); and (3) some degree of rationing and price controls, and a lot more attention paid to cost effectiveness (what works versus what's wasteful).

Before anybody freaks out over the rationing part of #3, let's be clear: Our current system rations like crazy. It's called *price* rationing, and there are 47 million uninsured people who'd be happy to discuss it with you.

So, that's why these countries spend one-half to two-thirds the share of GDP that we spend on health care, but cover everyone and still manage to report generally better health outcomes on important stuff like lower infant mortality rates, longer life expectancy, and less obesity, diabetes, and hypertension.

The absence of large risk pools and the inefficiencies in the private market are not the only reasons we spend a lot more for less. Pretty much everything I've told you thus far is well known, but moving to universal coverage would not, on its own, solve our other health care problem: the fact that health care spending is outpacing the growth of the overall economy. Every year, we're spending more and more as a share of our economy on health care. Less than half of the increase is due to the aging of the population—it's mostly due to increases in medical costs, which year after year outpace overall inflation.

So how do we wrestle these costs down? I'm afraid it's another case of the need to do battle with a powerful foe—in this case, the medical industrial complex. Sure, expensive technologies are desirable—jeez, who wouldn't want his kid to get a CAT scan when she bumped her head?—but a careful look at the way we spend health dollars suggests lots of waste and profiteering in the name of "good medicine," something I go into in greater detail below and in Chapter 5.

Crunchpoint: It's true. Every other modern economy delivers health care to more people with better results at less cost, and they do so by at least partially "de-commoditizing" health care: To one degree or another, they take it out of the market. This doesn't mean it will be costless to follow their lead. When we fix this, and I think we may to be poised to take a serious run at it, some folks will receive less health care than they do today. But many others will receive more, and if we get it right, we'll all benefit from the establishment of a system that covers everyone and does so in a way that doesn't metastasize into an inoperable tumor.

Why is our health care system so crazy expensive, yet my health insurance company won't pay for all of my child's routine medical checkups?

To paraphrase slightly, why does our nation spend lavishly on all kinds of pricey care but skimp on routine prevention? Here's a place where old-fashioned economic analysis is pretty helpful: Follow the incentives. Beware, though. The path they lead you down is not pretty.

Most health coverage is based on deductibles and premiums. Once you've paid your share—the deductible—the premium kicks in and the insurer takes over. Cheap plans offer high deductibles: You pay comparatively little for the plan, but it doesn't kick in until you've shelled out some serious bucks. Sounds good if you're healthy. But that's risky. You might not be as healthy as you think, and if some serious accident or illness befalls you, you're both sick and screwed.

On the other hand, if you have the dough, you can buy an expensive plan that kicks in with coverage quickly. But remember, these insurers weren't born yesterday. You as much as cough while you're filling out the form, and there's no way they're going to cover your sickly butt, even with an expensive plan.

Most of us with coverage end up somewhere in the middle, but once we're no longer paying the bulk of our costs, we don't have a great incentive to conserve. I know I've argued against many basic economic precepts in these pages, but in this case, I'm with the textbooks: Price signals matter. It's true that, like this questioner's kid, we underconsume preventive care. But at the same time, many of us overconsume wasteful and inefficient health care. Why? Because we don't face the real costs.

Health policy analyst Ezra Klein uses this metaphor to describe the problem: "You eat more at a buffet because the refills are free, and you use more health care because insurers generally make you pay up front in premiums, rather than at the point of care."[21]

But it's even a little worse. There's an episode of *The Simpsons* in which Homer bankrupts an all-you-can-eat seafood restaurant. The buffet idea works for the restaurant because they can count on most diners' getting full. With health care, we're more like Homer, going back for ever-more-expensive treatments and drug regimens with no mechanism to satiate our infinite demand for health.

The insurers fight back with everything from hassle factors (making you or your doc jump through hoops to get reimbursed), to co-pays (you shell out 10 bucks at the MD's office or the pharmacy), to covering two "well baby" visits this year as opposed to three last year.

Let me be clear about this last glib point regarding the baby visits, lest I'm accused of falling into the same "More health care is always better health care" assumption that's partially gotten us into this mess. It may be that two well-baby visits are all that the typical baby needs to remain healthy, and while more visits might be reassuring to Mom and Dad, that's precisely the kind of waste we need to drive out of the system. The question is, who makes that call? If it's the insurer, forgive us—me and the person asking this question—if we're a bit skeptical regarding the insurer's ability to objectively do so.

At any rate, the insurers have been highly successful in the sense that their profits have been robust,[22] but that's partly because they've been raising costs: Premiums since 2000 have been growing at a rate that's more than three times that of overall inflation. Family coverage premiums were up 67 percent from 2000 to 2005, compared with 13 percent for overall inflation.

Who pays these costs? Our employers do, but so do we, through lower wages and higher prices. American cars, for example, cost more than those of our competitors who don't face these irrational burdens. The fast-rising cost of health care is one reason for the squeeze I write about elsewhere, as employers move that raise you expected out of your paycheck and into your insurer's pocket.[23] More and more, we pay through greater direct payments into the health care system, as employers shift costs back to their workers.

OK, you say. But we're getting something for all that money, right?

Well, sure, we're getting lots of health care, but it's not making us any healthier than those much cheaper systems would. Well-known studies show that, controlling for how healthy or sick people are, health outcomes do not differ based on how much treatment people receive. One study by the Rand Corporation is particularly instructive because it followed people who were randomly sorted into insurance plans with great variation in their generosity (the random sorting is key, because you want the sick people and the healthies randomly distributed among the plans). As you would expect, those in the Cadillac plans got a lot more care, 40 percent more than those driving Hyundais. But their health outcomes were unaffected. (Important exception: The poor in the more generous plans fared better than the poor in cheaper plans, because—news flash—they tend to underconsume health care.)

Some findings suggest weird regional differences. For example, in certain parts of the country, C-sections are a lot more likely (for no apparent reason); and elderly persons in their last stages of life will see many more specialists in one part of the country relative to another—again, with no difference in outcome.[24] By default, people across the country are, at their doctors' behest, getting expensive and exotic tests just because they're there, with no regard to their cost effectiveness.

As Ezra Klein summarizes in his *American Prospect* article, "Not only is more care not always better, it is sometimes worse—and it is *always* more expensive."[25] The nonpartisan wonks of the Congressional Budget Office (CBO), who crunch the budget numbers for the Congress, are duly freaked out about the longer-term budgetary implications of these developments and echo Klein's point in their own starchy terms: "Significant evidence exists that more-expensive care need not mean higher-quality care—suggesting an opportunity to reduce costs without impairing health outcomes."[26]

Here's a revealing picture about this story from the CBO. Each dot represents a state, and they plot the relationship between a quality of care measure on the y-axis and that state's per-beneficiary Medicare costs (x-axis).[27] If costs and quality were correlated, the dots would generally line up from the lower left to the upper right of the figure. Instead,

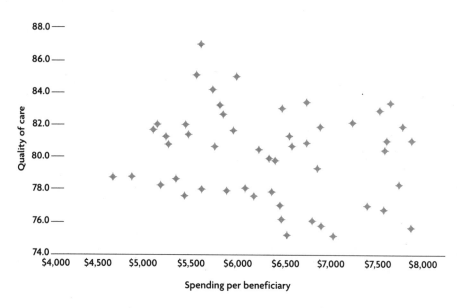

Figure 1.2. Spending and quality of care for Medicare beneficiaries, with each dot representing a state. Do you see a relationship? (I see a little doggie . . .). (Source: *Health Care and Budget: Issues and Challenges for Reform*, Congressional Budget Office, June 21, 2007 [figure 4].)

they're randomly scattered about. I kind of see a little doggie running, but that's me. I also see some pretty obvious waste. We're clearly kickin' back, spending money hand over fist, with little regard for what works, and for what's cost effective and what's not.

Given the nature of the problem, stopping this waste has been and will continue to be extremely hard. Who wants to be the one whose spouse, child, or parent doesn't get the fancy drug because it might not be "cost effective"? Our own infinite demand for anything we think might help us or our loved ones is but one of the intractable forces we're up against. The other is the MdIC.

There's no better critic of the MdIC than health policy analyst Merrill Goozner, a guy who not only has fearlessly looked in every dark corner of that complex, but also has the medical knowledge to recognize waste when he sees it.[28] Here's how he sees the fight we need to have:

In [these] debates, we'll be taking on the drug, device, and durable equipment makers, the diagnostic testing industry, hospitals and organized medicine, as well as the tobacco industry, environmental polluters, the food industry and other drivers of poor health in American society.[29]

Those are some pretty formidable foes, but here is the reason why we as a society must join this fight: Something's got to give. The arithmetic is, once again, scarily simple. If spending on health care keeps growing faster than our income, the share of our economy devoted to health care will continue to rise.

Some economists have argued that they're OK with that. We are an aging, rich country, and, as I've been stressing, spending on health care is, to introduce a tiny bit of useful jargon, "highly elastic," meaning that as our income goes up, we want more, more, more of it. In this view, we're sovereign consumers buying lots of what we want. That's the genius of the market, right?

Uhh . . . nope. We're consumers who are pretty much helpless to recognize the utility of what's being proffered, whether it's a $5,000 screw for our hip joint or an MRI for a headache. Some of those screws and MRIs will be tremendously life enhancing, if not livesaving, but we don't know which ones, and the system is set up to keep us from learning or caring about the difference. And, to be fair, a lot of well-intentioned doctors don't know, either. That way, the bucks keep flowing to the MdIC.

There's got to be a better way. Read on.

Crunchpoint: Health care in America costs so much because consumers don't face the costs, we tend to have insatiable demands, and no one in charge is trying to figure out what works and what's wasteful—meaning that quality and cost have far too little to do with each other. Fixing these structural problems puts us on a collision course with the medical industrial complex, and those guys are street fighters (K Street, that is).

What's it going to take for large-scale health reform to occur?

This is a tricky question to answer because a large majority of us, according to health care expert Atul Gawande, are satisfied with our own coverage and care.[30] The problems discussed above are real, but their result is more of a slow bleed than a hemorrhage, so my answer—and this is clearly more about politics than economics—is that change is going to come only gradually. We'll get to large-scale reform, but it will occur through chaining together a bunch of small-scale steps. We won't see Medicare for All anytime soon, but we might see it for selected age groups, like children or those nearing retirement.

That said, I'm confident that reform will occur, and let me quickly

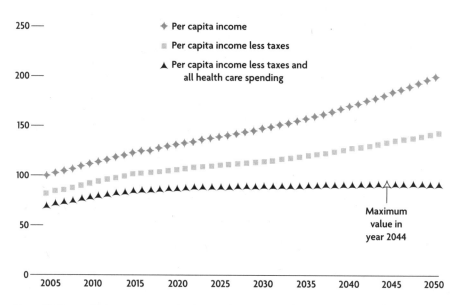

Figure 1.3. Per capita income, per capita income less taxes, and per capita income less taxes and all health care spending, 2005–2050. (Source: Henry Aaron, Brookings Institution, used with permission from Mr. Aaron.)

shift back to my economics turf to show you a convincing picture of why I think so. It relates closely to principle #3, regarding trade-offs, the notion that economics often forces us to choose one thing over something else. The trajectory of health care spending, both private and public, is going to be forcing our hand in this regard in a big way, and not all that far down the road.

The figure captures two critical points. First, excess health spending is not simply a public sector problem, as in, we can fix Medicare and be done with it. It's a private sector problem, too. In fact, it's worse there, which is the figure's second point: The current rate of health care spending will, in a few decades, leave us with a lot less disposable income.

The top line shows that real GDP per person is expected to double over the next 50 or so years. Sounds good, right? We'll all be wealthier, at least on average.

Not so fast. The next line shows that if we account for the taxes we'll need to pay for public health care, like Medicare and Medicaid (along with other stuff, but those are the big-ticket items), real income will start lower and grow more slowly. But it's still up about 75 percent, meaning once we pay for public health care, we're still better off over time.

But it's the bottom line that's the nasty one. Here we take out private sector health care spending, under the assumption that nothing changes in the way we spend these dollars. Income growth peaks in 2044 and we're actually poorer than we would be otherwise after that. And this is "per capita," or average, income. Excuse me if I worry that those in the bottom half will get whacked the hardest.

Now, I distrust 50-year forecasts as much as you probably do, so don't take these future trends as indisputable. But do view them as a hard-headed warning against blithely following the current path, nudged happily along our way by economic positivists jabbering about "sovereign consumers exercising their preferences."

Even if we wanted to, we could not continue down that path, a fact that's widely known and appreciated by policymakers of all stripes, as well as by the MdIC itself. As we near the point where income minus the cost of health care flattens or even falls, excessive, wasteful health spending inexorably crowds out our ability to invest in or pay for other stuff we want and need. We will be unable to improve schools, get more low and middle-income kids through college, make the needed investments to push back global warming, or simply make the paycheck go far enough to meet basic needs and aspirations.

And even if you think your family's health care plan is OK, at some point that squeeze will get your attention. It's already gotten the attention of some of the states. As is often the case with big policy matters in the United States, the states tend to act before the feds, and some big players, including California and Massachusetts, are not waiting for Big Brother to get started. They and others are trying out good ideas, mostly involving "pay or play" plans: Employers either provide coverage to their workers or pay into a state plan to do so.

This phenomenon where states serve as laboratories for what later becomes national policy has a pretty good track record, but there are reasons to be a little skeptical in this case. First, remember all that stuff about the benefits of a large risk pool? Well, certain states have a disadvantage in this regard, like Florida and Arizona, with their larger-than-average share of elderly residents and low-income immigrants.

But a bigger constraint is fiscal: States just don't have as deep and flexible a purse as the feds. Unlike the federal government, states have to balance their budgets, meaning that in economic hard times, when revenue grows scarce, they'll have to start cutting health services, and this at a time when folks are particularly vulnerable. We've actually seen this happen already, around a public health insurance program for children that's funded by a combination of state and fed bucks. States generously expanded coverage in the flush 1990s and retrenched in the 2000s.

So, while we should look closely at the state experiments and learn all we can from them, one lesson seems to be that you can't do this effectively at the state level. You need the big elephant (more likely, the big donkey) in the ring.

Crunchpoint: The current health care system—public and private—can't be sustained, in the sense that it will soon start gobbling up too much of our income to be justified, especially considering the unsatisfactory outcomes. Change is a-comin', but it's likely to be incremental. That's fine, as long as the baby steps we're taking are on the right path, toward single-payer coverage and away from the MdIC.

■ My health plan betrays me.
I fight alone
against a stronger foe.

How many people are actually poor in America?

As of this writing, the most recent poverty statistics inform us that there were 36.5 million officially poor people in the United States in 2006, 12.3 percent of the population.[31] They're "official" in the sense that they meet the government definition, but we hit a snag right away: Not even the officials believe the official measure. It's terribly out of date and is simply no longer a reliable measure of economic deprivation. Even the statistician who invented our poverty measure lo these 40 years ago doesn't believe it anymore.[32]

Let's take a quick look at how we measure poverty and why the measure has become so inadequate. For you to be counted as officially poor, your income gets compared with a threshold for your family size. For example, for a family with two parents and two kids, the 2006 threshold was about $20,400; for a single parent with two kids, the threshold was about $16,200. If your family income, with a few adjustments, was below that level, you were poor.[33]

The official thresholds were based on food costs of low-income families in the mid-1950s. Surveys showed that these families spent about a third of their income on food, so we simply tripled the value of the "economy food plan" (the cheapest nutritionally adequate food plan derived by the Department of Agriculture[34]) for a given family size.

Amazingly, with very few changes and with adjustments for inflation, this remains the official poverty measure to this day. Food consumption represents a much smaller share of family budgets than was the case 50 years ago (its average share has fallen by about half),[35] while housing, transportation, and health care, for example, constitute larger shares. Simply updating the official thresholds for this change alone would lead poverty thresholds (and poverty rates) to be much higher today.

But there's a deeper problem with the official approach: As living standards rise for the rest of society, those deemed poor by a fixed income level that is adjusted solely for price changes will fall behind the rest of us. Back in 1960, the official poverty threshold for a family of four was about half the typical (median) income for a four-person family. Today, it's around 30 percent of the four-person median.

In an era with sharply growing income inequality, it is worth contemplating the importance of this development. Why should we be concerned if our poverty thresholds drift farther below the income of the median household?

The answer is that the concept of deprivation is not solely an absolute concept; it is a relative one as well. Economists since Adam (Smith, that is) have recognized that even if the poor are able to meet their fundamental needs for food and shelter in such a way to sustain their lives, they can, by dint of the economic and social distance between themselves and the rest of us, still experience deprivation that is harmful to society.

As Smith put it, over 200 years ago:

> By necessaries I understand not only the commodities which are indispensably necessary for the support of life, but what ever the customs of the country renders it indecent for creditable people, even the lowest order, to be without. A linen shirt, for example, is, strictly speaking, not a necessary of life. The Greeks and Romans lived, I suppose, very comfortably, though they had no linen. But in the present times, through the greater part of Europe, a creditable day-laborer would be ashamed to appear in public without a linen shirt, the want of which would be supposed to denote that disgraceful degree of poverty which, it is presumed, nobody can well fall into, without extreme bad conduct. Custom, in the same manner, has rendered leather shoes a necessary of life in England.[36]

In other words, whether or not you're poor isn't simply a matter of whether you can afford to meet your most basic needs. It's also a question of whether you're keeping up with the general rise in living standards that most people are experiencing and enjoying.

To this day, top-tier poverty analysts who should know better overlook this point, citing material gains made by today's poor relative to those of the past. Two such analysts, for example, writing in 1999, noted, "By the standards of 1971, many of today's poor families might be considered members of the middle class."[37] Another noted that "poor people's physical and material well-being is considerably better now than in the late '60s. How else to explain why so many poor now have color TV (93%) and air conditioning (50%), and own their own homes (46%)?"[38]

Such comparisons implicitly freeze the well-being of the poor at a point in time, ignoring progress in technology, consumption, relative prices, and opportunities. In short, to ignore the economic distance between the poor and everyone else is to ensure that they will remain outside the mainstream. Yes, they will not starve, many will be housed, and they will all watch TV in color. But they will still be separate and unequal relative to the majority.

Does all this mean we don't know how many poor people there are today? Fear not, poverty warriors: the faithful Census Bureau has been working hard on improving the measure. An updated measure that corrects for many of the shortcomings of the official one would add another 4.5 million to the poverty rolls.[39] Were it not for political constraints—no president wants to add that many people to the rolls on his watch—we would retire the old measure and adopt the new one.

Crunchpoint: Though we do a lousy job of measuring it, there are a lot of poor people in America, about 40 million in the mid-2000s. Yet all is far from lost in the war on poverty. Read on.

■ **Counting the poor?**
Would it not be better to
Simply help them aboard?

OK, I'm glad we could do a better job measuring poverty. I'm sure that makes you social scientists very happy. But how about ending it? Couldn't we just put an end to poverty if we gave the poor a little money?

No, we couldn't really end poverty just by giving the poor a little money. I mean, we could, but (a) it would cost $62 billion a year, and (b) it's not going to end poverty. Poverty in America is not just a lack of resources, although, as I stress in the next question, that tends to be the poor's most pressing problem. What sustains poverty is the lack of educational and employment opportunities, along with a lack of ongoing supports to give people the lift they need.

How do I know that? Lots of academic research, for one, but more convincing is the fact that for a few years in the 1990s, we provided the poor and near-poor with what was missing, and the results were dramatic, as we'll see in a moment.

But why are they poor? As you might expect, we've been arguing about that forever. When the first poor person stumbled into the marketplace, an argument broke out as to whether it was his fault for being a lazy bum with low morals or society's fault for not providing him with adequate opportunities. In the economic debate, this reduces to whether you believe unfettered market forces or government solutions can fix the poverty problem.

The argument will never end, because it's too reductionist. As we learned in the 1990s, it takes both forces working together. During those years, we made a huge dent in our poverty problem, and the main causes were the tightest labor market in 30 years and a new, beefed-up set of antipoverty policies.

Some of these policies were delivered under the rubric of welfare reform, a mid-1990s change in poverty policy that had some harsh, punitive aspects but also invested some serious resources in "work supports," programs that help poor people move into the workforce and stay there for a while.

We increased worker training and access to higher education; added child care, health care, housing, and transportation subsidies; implemented a major expansion of the Earned Income Tax Credit, a program that adds literally thousands of dollars to the incomes of working poor parents (around $4,500 for a family with at least two kids in 2007); and raised the minimum wage.

At the same time that welfare reform and work supports were pushing poor people into work, the job market pulled them in. In the latter 1990s, the labor market heated up more than it had in 30 years, and as unemployment began to slide down, even low-wage employers had to raise wage offers to get and keep the workers they needed.

It was the perfect resolution to the irresolvable historical poverty argument—market and nonmarket forces working together to solve a problem neither could solve alone—and the results were striking. Figure 1.4 shows the depressingly high poverty rates of African-American children from 1979 to 2006.[40] The rate basically cruised along in the mid-40s throughout the 1980s, despite the ongoing economic recovery in those years, a recovery that clearly bypassed poor black families.

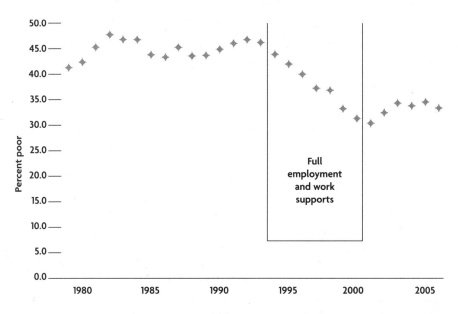

Figure 1.4. Poverty rates, African-American children: We got it right for a minute. (Source: U.S. Census Bureau.)

But from 1992 to 2000, thanks to increased jobs and earnings for African-Americans, black child poverty rates fell an unprecedented 17 percentage points, from 47 to 30 percent. Granted, ending up with about one-third of African-American kids in poverty isn't exactly a huge success story, but we'll never get child poverty down to the levels we want if we don't get the trend headed in the right direction. And, man, it was definitely doing that.

But with the 2001 recession, the trend stalled. This, too, is elucidative: There were no policy changes in that year, but you need both policy and markets pointing in the right direction, and when the market dropped out, poverty headed north again. In fact, it became clear in those years that with all our policy emphasis on work supports, we'd lost some of the safety net functions that poor people need when work disappears.[41]

We've never regained the full-employment conditions that prevailed in the latter 1990s, and poverty rose through 2005 (poverty fell slightly, from 12.6 percent to 12.3 percent in 2006; that left it one point above its 2000 level and added 4.9 million to the ranks of the poor).

Crunchpoint: We can't end poverty by giving money to poor people because it doesn't scratch the itch that keeps them poor. For years, scholars argued whether that itch should be scratched by government or markets. Thanks to critical lessons learned in the 1990s, we know it's both: When market forces deliver a full-employment job market, and publicly provided work supports help to close the deal, we can make tremendous progress against poverty.

Should I give money to the guy selling the "Street Sheet" outside my office?

Sure. It helps chip away at his most pressing problem—poverty. But it's a very temporary fix.

Economists worry about negative incentives, which in this case is the idea that you could inculcate dependency by supporting this marginal enterprise. In fact, the "Street Sheet" was invented in part to avoid the pure begging done by destitute people (usually men). Giving money to that person feels a little different, and that's probably because even the most liberal among us worry about fostering damaging incentives. But the guy selling the "Street Sheet" is something of an entrepreneur. Still, the main question here from an economic perspective is, does your contribution help or hurt this guy?

Is he more likely to look for a legit job, or at least one with steady hours and more reliable pay, if nobody gives him anything? The research that gets closest to this suggests that there's a small chance that he might, if he were mentally up to it and if such work were available to him. But this whole dependency rap has been way overplayed. Conservatives argued for years that welfare payments kept people from seeking work, and while the statistical evidence suggested that there was something to that, the effects were economically small. That is, in the absence of welfare benefits, the evidence was that poor people would work just a little bit more than they did already.

Most of this research was on single mothers. In the 1980s, when we experimented with ending welfare payments for single men ("general assistance" was the term of art), the research didn't show that such payments were what stood between these men and gainful employment.

The real barriers turned out to be their own personal limitations, in terms of skills and in some cases mental illness, and the lack of decent jobs for people with limited skills and an unimpressive work history.

For parents, especially single parents, the lack of reliable and safe child-care options just made things worse. In the 1990s, welfare reform turned a lot of this around, but in many ways, the successes of that program—more solid labor market connections, lower poverty rates—have been misunderstood.

By "welfare reform," I mean a big set of legal changes in the rules governing the receipt of welfare benefits, along with an equally important set of attitudinal changes in the way the program was administered on the ground level. The rule changes made work in the paid labor market a much greater requirement of benefit receipt. The ground-level changes meant those administering the program were much less quick to just hand over and send the recipient on her way.

Some argue that the lesson of welfare reform is that once welfare benefits were contingent upon finding a job, people got their act together and went to work. Which, if true, might lead you to start stiffing the guy outside your office. Give him an incentive to find real work, and he'll do so. But that's not what went on in those years.

For example, you might think we spent less on welfare in those years (the 1990s), and we certainly spent a lot less on welfare benefits. But the fact is, we ended up spending tens of billions more helping the poor move from welfare to work, subsidizing their wages and providing them with so-called work supports, such as subsidies for child and health care, transportation and other costs of work, and worker training. And while these efforts gave the recipients an added push, the pull of the strongest low-wage labor market in 30 years also helped (see the full-employment discussion in Chapter 5 for more discussion).

Years ago, I was a social worker in New York City's East Harlem, where I met all kinds of people needing all kinds of help. But I'll tell you the two things that most of these people had in common. First, they lacked economic resources, and that made everything so much harder for them, from getting a phone turned on, to keeping a roof overhead, to getting themselves or their kids some health care (to this day, I remember an entire day spent trying to get someone in chronic pain in to see a dentist). Second, their economic aspirations were the same as everyone else's.

If you think I'm being sentimental, you're wrong. Maybe it's a "selection bias"—these folks came for help—but when I think back on my clients from those long-ago days, my impression is of people pretty much just like me but (a) persons of color and (b) intensely hassled with the challenges of making ends meet and parenting their kids. Many also were worried, if not depressed, by the nagging fear that they were not doing right by their kids, whom they feared were not getting the opportunities they deserved.

Which is simply to say that the guy selling the "Street Sheet" is most likely trying to get by the best way he knows. Would he be better off with a stable job with a decent wage and health coverage? Are folks living and/or working on the street more likely to have all kinds of problems, with drug abuse and possibly a criminal record at the top of the list? Of course, in both cases. But does your dollar somehow make his goals less attainable or his problems worse?

To the contrary, his most immediate problem is poverty, and your dollar helps chip away at that, so feel free to give it up.

Crunchpoint: The biggest problem facing the "Street Sheet" seller and others like him is society's reluctance to invest in their well-being. Your dollar helps in the very short run, and all that negative-incentive stuff has been way overplayed. But what he really needs is the political support for an agenda that helps folks like him get into the legit economy, an agenda I present in Chapter 5.

Why do teachers make so little compared with stock traders? Aren't the teachers entrusted with greater responsibilities?

Economists have an answer to this that's as simple as it is unsatisfying: People are paid what they're worth. That is, they are paid according to the value they add to the economy.

It's your classic, pristine economic assumption: If, by definition, you're paid according to your "value added," you cannot, by definition, be under- or overpaid. If you think you're earning too little, then you must be placing an inflated value on your self-worth. Your economic self-esteem is too high.

How do I know this is wrong? Oh, come on . . . can't I just assert it? Does anyone really believe that people are paid their precise worth? How come other people get to make bogus assumptions and I've gotta prove everything?!

(Sorry—excuse the rant. We're back live.)

Contradictions abound, in fact. People doing a job in high-end firms get paid more than those doing the same job in low-end ones, like janitors at Goldman Sachs versus those at the dockside warehouse. Union workers make more than nonunion workers doing the same job. Even when we control for all the relevant differences (experience, occupation, education), women and minorities earn less than white men (and 75 percent of public school teachers are women). Most recently, earnings have stagnated—the real weekly earnings of the typical (median) worker were down slightly between 2000 and 2006.[42] Yet the economy's productivity rose 17 percent. There is simply, absolutely, unequivocally no way that people were being paid commensurate with their contributions to the economy over those years.

Not that there's no relationship between value added and earnings, but a million other factors come into play. Let's examine a few regarding the question posed above.

First, the motivation behind this question is usually something like: "Teachers are educating our future citizens and workforce, while stock traders are making bets that Ukrainian oil futures will fall relative to Bulgarian wheat prices. Shouldn't society value the former more than the latter?"

Well, part of what determines your pay in occupations like law, finance, and real estate, for example, is the money you bring in through the door. Successful traders bring in a lot; successful teachers don't bring in any. So, part of the answer is that traders and lawyers and such folks are literally working with the coin of the realm. Valuing teachers' work, which is really more like valuing an investment, takes a little more thought.

How, in fact, should we evaluate teachers' "output"? The rage nowadays is to hold teachers and schools accountable for test scores. While this sounds like a reasonable metric, there are countless factors that affect a student's ability to learn, and some of the most important ones are at work outside the realm of education and inside the realm of family.

And even if we could have faith in such output measures and they led us to believe we should pay teachers more, where would that lead us? Right to the taxpayer.

Herein lies the other rub. Teachers, at least the majority of the K-12 ones who work in the public sector, get paid through taxes, mostly local ones. And that can be a terribly tough wedge between what you get and what you're worth. Communities are constantly squabbling over this issue, and if you've ever been to a town meeting, you know how contentious this gets. Those asking taxpayers to pony up more bucks for teacher pay can't point to a new library, a ball field, or another such structure. They've got to make the case that this is the right investment.

Teachers' unions get villainized, and you can find examples where lousy teachers were unduly protected by the union. But all of the above discussion tells you why you really need unions here: Without them, the teachers would have little bargaining clout against those who would devalue their work. To the contrary, let us not forget principle #1, regarding the role of power in determining economic outcomes. We should thank the unions for trying to keep teachers' pay high enough to attract decent people to the job.

And, in fact, in terms of compensation, the unions aren't as successful as their detractors make them out to be. Careful research shows that we underpay teachers. Even accounting for the fact that most of them work fewer hours per year than comparably skilled professionals (that is, controlled for education, age, and other relevant characteristics), when we compare their pay with that of other such workers, they earn less than they should.[43]

Crunchpoint: We underpay teachers because we undervalue their work. This is partly because, despite the great responsibilities they shoulder, it's not easy to value their output, compared with that of other professions, and partly because they're paid through taxes, and it's always a struggle to convince taxpayers that they need to pay more for something, especially when the returns are down the road.

Should we aspire to a totally equal society? Is there anything good about inequality?

I get this one a lot, and it gives me a chance to underscore an important point that can get lost in all this inveighing against the extent of inequality in today's economy. Inequality is inherent in economies, modern and ancient. While some utopians might aspire to total equality, I don't, and it's not happening in our lifetime, anyway.

The classic response to this question, usually by those who would like to downplay the extent to which income and wealth have become concentrated at the top, is that we seek equality of opportunity, not of outcomes. Everyone should have an equal chance to attend a top school or enter a profession for which they're qualified, for example, but no one should be guaranteed that their grades or pay will be equal to those of others. That's for the "market" to decide, based on individual merit.

Now, that's a perfectly fine, albeit pretty abstract, goal. But the problem is, the distribution of opportunity follows that of wealth. When too many economic resources are held by too few, when the benefits of growth elude broad swaths of working families, opportunity itself becomes a rare commodity, out of the reach of the majority. Too much inequality precludes a meritocracy. We see this most clearly in educational opportunity, where college-completion rates for high-score poor kids are about equal to those of low-score rich kids.[44]

In *crunch* terms, I've stressed how excessively unequal economic outcomes hurt living standards and aspirations, but there's a political price to pay here, too, and it can be steep. If people feel that the system is rigged against them, they're less invested in that system. The first sign is political disengagement, and we've certainly seen that relative to other countries with more narrow income distributions. But the next stage is one I also try to warn about in these pages: opposition to positive aspects of free markets that people perceive as hostile to their economic interests, such as globalization and immigration.

It is precisely for this reason that capitalism always comes with pressure valves— policies and social norms devised explicitly to preclude the excesses of wealth and power concentration that threaten the system. The fact that these "excess dampeners" have withered is one of the reasons for our current difficulties, and therefore the policy set I introduce later is designed largely with one intention: to bring them back to life. Resetting America's economic balance must become our central policy goal in this area.

The other part of the question—is inequality ever good?—is also interesting. Some level of inequality is a fact of life, one I don't view as particularly good or bad. But this does give me a chance to warn of a strange and misguided argument I've seen surface in conservative and libertarian circles: Inequality is *very* good, because it creates strong incentives.

The idea here is that fast-growing inequality makes the returns to success and penalties of failure much greater. You've more to gain and more to lose, so you try harder. Sounds like a dark mixture of Machiavelli and Darwin to me, but I suppose it's plausible. In real life, however, it appears to be just plain wrong.

Though surely market incentives affect effort, this idea takes that notion to a silly extreme, one for which there's no evidence. There have never been signs of greater effort in periods of high levels of inequality. If anything, the opposite has occurred, as the have-nots drop out of a game they perceived to be rigged against them, and the haves, content that the game in rigged in their favor, chill by the swimming pool (that's just snark—the rich work a lot, but their effort is uncorrelated with inequality). Some interesting behavioral research has shown that the inequality incentive structure does have one noticeable impact: It leads insiders to cheat more, because they figure the system is tilted their way anyway, so who'll notice if they cut a corner?[45] Call it the Halliburton effect.

A recent variant of this "greed is good" motif has been applied to college attendance. Some prominent economists, including Nobel laureate

Gary Becker, claim that high inequality sends a market signal to high school grads that they should attend college.[46] They even go so far as to oppose progressive tax changes as a move that would dampen people's incentives to get more education. Raising taxes on wealthy people, in their model, would be advocating "a tax on going to college and a subsidy for dropping out of high school."

These scholars really believe that some kid who's considering going to college today will think, "I was seriously looking at college. But, hey, a few decades from now, I could be making serious bucks, and if the 2010 Congress is just going let the high-end marginal tax rates reset from 35 to 39.6 percent, what's the point? I hear Starbucks is hiring."

Or, even more bizarre, some kid thinking about dropping out of high school will allegedly say, "Jeez, a Democrat could win in '08, and they're talking about letting tax rates on capital gains and dividend income go back up. Relative to rich people, that lowers my tax bill . . . I'm so outta here!"

I'm not making this up. In mid-2007, these economists put forth this argument as a reason we'd better not let the Bush high-end tax cuts phase out as planned.

Perhaps you've got to be a Nobelist in economics to be able to convince yourself that people need a rising after-tax wage premium to persuade them to go to college. You've also got to ignore the fact that other countries with much less inequality have college graduation rates at least as high as ours, and in fact, these countries have seen much faster advances in college attainment than we have.[47]

If you ask me, that's what these big shots should be concerned about. I've looked at our lagging higher-ed attainment problem, and the most obvious cause seems to be a diminished ability among those in the bottom half of the income scale to afford the price tag of higher education. In other words, it's exactly the opposite of what the economists are telling us: Inequality is not promoting college attendance—the crunch is discouraging it.

These economists also could have looked at the fact that the largest spurt in college attendance occurred in the 1970s, having nothing to do with the relative wage advantage of college over high school workers, which fell in those years. It was instead a combination of the baby boomers' entering their college years and the fact that college students got draft deferrals from the Vietnam War. Now there's an example of incentives at work.

Crunchpoint: Once you get as close to equal opportunity as you can, some degree of unequal outcomes is neither bad nor good. It's excessive inequality that's a problem, particularly when the benefits of growth elude those responsible for generating that growth. Our economy used to have mechanisms to preclude such excesses, but they are broken and need fixing . . . fast.

The one thing all economists seem to agree on is that the best if not the only way out of this squeeze is for more people to get more education. Sounds simple and makes sense. But is it right?

No, it's not right. A more highly educated society is obviously a better society, but more education will not solve all or even most of our economic problems.

Economists and the policymakers who listen to them often end up confusing people on this point, because they default to it in every case. That is, I've seen politicians tell aging industrial workers that they need a college education to compete in the global economy. Now, there's no question in my mind that most of the time, a more highly educated worker has a real competitive advantage over one with less schooling, but it's simply unrealistic and far too simplistic to think that everyone is going to get more schooling.

Do you know what share of our workforce is college educated—that is, has at least a four-year degree? It's about 30 percent.[48] Is it really possible that we have an economy structured to function effectively for only about a third of us?

In fact, it's not possible. Thankfully, we have an economy that generates a great deal of labor demand for workers with all kinds of educational credentials, including those with very few.

Often, the image of the skill demands for the types of jobs we create are quite skewed in the minds of many economists and policymakers. They tend to envision white-coated "symbolic analysts" who are pointing and clicking the way forward, uncovering the nanotech secrets that will drive the next economic revolution. And, in fact, a tiny share of the workforce—way less than half a percent—does exactly that. But these folks also need someone to mind their kids while they're designing the future, someone to wash and fold the lab coat, and someone to prep the food they'll pick up on the way home.

If you look at the current and future composition of jobs (the Bureau of Labor Statistics has a pretty good track record predicting future job categories), you'll find that the sectors adding the most jobs are cashiers, food prep, nurses, home health aides, security guards, waiters and waitresses, customer service reps, landscapers, and truck drivers. In fact, looking at the top 20 occupations expected to add the most jobs over the next 10 years, you've got to get to number 19 before you find an image to match the conventional wisdom.[49] There you will find computer software engineers, right in between truckers and repair/maintenance workers.

By the way, there's an interesting characteristic that ties many of these job categories together: They can't be moved to offshore destinations. A waitress in Bangalore can't serve your burger in Cleveland. You've got to be in the hotel to make the bed and prep the food. This is another factor militating against the "Education is everything" mindset. Jobs at all skill levels are in competition in the global economy, and even if everyone became a PhD tomorrow, many of the challenges I write about in this book would still be operative.[50]

These changes imply an interesting new development in our economy: Inequality's growth is now driven less by educational differences than by competition between select people in the right place at the right time with the right assets, regardless of skills. In mid-2007, this phenomenon made the front page of the *New York Times*, in an article documenting "the growing concentration of wealth and income among a select group at the pinnacle of success, *leaving many others with similar talents and experience well behind*" (my italics).[51]

Take a look, for example, at what happened to the incomes of the very rich households in the top 1 percent of the income scale (average income in 2005: $1.1 mil) and those of the "only pretty rich" households just below them (those between the 90th and 99th percentiles—average income: $151K).[52] Clearly, we're comparing the haves with the have-mores here, a largely college-educated group, so any difference between them is not explained by a conventional education/skills story.

Between 2001 and 2005, the average income of the "pretty rich" group grew a measly 3 percent after inflation, while that of the top 1 percent was up 23 percent. Accordingly, the income gap between these two groups rose as well, with the top 1 percent having 6.5 times the income as the 90 to 99 percent group in 2005, up from 6.2 times in 2001 and way above the 3.7 multiple at the end of the 1970s.[53]

All of that said, it's absolutely legitimate for policymakers to stress the benefits of greater skills and more education. I think it's so important that I devote a section to this challenge in Chapter 5, wherein I focus on greater access to quality education for the disadvantaged. But with the majority of the workforce not college educated, and with lots of demand for their lower- and middle-level skills, shouldn't we also worry about the quality of the jobs that these people will face today, tomorrow, and even in the long term?

Of course we should. But we won't if we're single-mindedly focused on educational upgrading. As a trained economist, I understand that bias firsthand. Our training and ideology allow us to think about the quality of inputs: We can legitimately argue for higher-quality labor and capital inputs into the "production function" (it's the magic box that combines the materials and skills [inputs] used to create goods and services [outputs]). But we're not supposed to wander over to issues of job quality, the fairness of wage levels, labor standards, or fringes like health and pension benefits, sick leave, overtime, and vacations. That's the purview of the pro-business politicians and U.S. Chamber of Commerce on one side, and labor unions on the other.

That prohibition must not stand. We are fully capable of holding two ideas in our minds: The best path for any individual is to get more skills, and the quality of existing and future jobs for folks at all skill levels matters a lot, too.

And there's also, of course, a political point in play here, one that relates to the first principle: power as a key determinant of economic outcomes. Behind the education exhortations of some policymakers, especially those who refuse to take any other actions to loosen the crunch, is a solidly "blame the victim" agenda. Earlier, I quoted a Bush official saying that it's up to the people "to take advantage of [the] opportunities" that the economy is creating.[54] In other words, it's not that we policymakers have a deficit of good ideas to promote broadly shared growth. It's that you, working person, suffer from a deficit of skills.

Let me assure you that there is absolutely no reason why someone with less than a college education can't enjoy consistent increases in his or her living standards in America today. There is nothing inherent in our economy or political system that would preclude that result, especially given the important role of such workers in our current and future labor markets. Yes, globalization will continue to displace some of these workers, now including those with relatively high levels of skills, and it will place downward pressure on the wage growth of many more others. Yet with a full-employment job market, the necessary forces in place to ensure adequate bargaining power (such as unions and decent minimum wage levels), and robust safety nets and social insurance—a policy set I elaborate upon in Chapter 5—all the bakers can get their fair slice of the pie.

Crunchpoint: The more education, the better. That's true for individuals and it's true for society. But it's not even close to a cure-all for the crunch. Economists and policymakers need to stop blaming the 70 percent of the workforce that's not college educated and start building the policy architecture to ensure that they too share in the growth of an economy to which their contributions are critical, not ancillary. The challenge is not just to make more people ready for skilled jobs. It's also to make more jobs ready for people regardless of their skill levels.

Don't Know Much About GDP

As a guy who never paid enough attention to professional sports—I love watching skilled athletes, but there are too many commercials and time-outs—to this day I get anxious and uncomfortable when people start talking about sports. For one, I don't know enough of the vernacular. (For example, pre-Google, I didn't know what a "triple-double" was in basketball. When I finally asked a friend, he was so convinced I was kidding that he wouldn't tell me.)[1]

A lot of people feel that way about economic terms of art, so this section presents the skinny on some of the biggies. Be forewarned: These are not Google or Wikipedia definitions. Along with the basics, I try to impart a sense of what these statistics reveal about how well our economy is working, and not necessarily from the perspective of the financial market analyst but rather from that of working families throughout the income scale.

My hope is to both guide you through a painless tour of ideas and concepts you've been dying to get under your belt—like what does GDP stand for, anyway? And what's up with the Federal Reserve?—and provide some commentary on how they relate to the three principles that frame much of our analysis.

hear a lot of talk about gross domestic product, or GDP. What is it? Should I get excited when it goes up and depressed when it doesn't?

GDP is the dollar value of the economy—sort of like what you'd have to pay for it if you wanted to buy it. It includes all the goods and services we buy, like cars, haircuts, health club memberships, books, lattes, and so on. It includes investments in factories, businesses, and homes. It includes government spending at all levels (federal, state, and local), and it includes net exports (the value of what we sell abroad minus what we buy from foreigners).

That much is standard accounting. Boring, I guess, but I still find our system of national accounts—the way we conceive of and track this stuff—to be a great intellectual triumph of economics (go to the U.S. Department of Commerce's Bureau of Economic Analysis Web site [http://www.bea.gov] to see the hundreds of tables with millions of data points that make up the national accounts; it's like a porn site for data nerds). What's interesting is what's left out.

First, it's "gross." Not as in "disgusting," but as in "not net." Thus, any spending we engage in shows up in GDP, even if it's to replace stuff that fell apart or was destroyed. This way of scoring growth can have a perverse effect: If there's a hurricane or a flood somewhere, chances are that place's GDP will show up as having grown because spending will increase there to replace what was lost. In 2005, the year of Hurricane Katrina, GDP was up 3.2 percent while net domestic product (*net* means gross minus stuff that was destroyed or used up) was up 2.5 percent.

Similarly, GDP often gets a big boost from wars, because we increase government spending to create arms and then often replace the stuff we use up. Were the Iraq War to end in 2007–08, defense contractors would still be billing the government for 10 years. That may not sound like productive spending, but it will show up as faster GDP growth.

GDP also fails to reflect environmental degradation. To the contrary, if you destroy coastal flood plains to develop a port, you boost GDP. You add more to GDP if you sell a fleet of expensive SUVs than if you sell a fleet of fuel-efficient but cheaper hybrids, because "gross" product doesn't deduct the environmental harm of the one versus the other. However, as discussed later, some farsighted economists are now taking seriously the economic threat to growth from global warming.

The national accounts—the nation's spreadsheets wherein we calculate all this stuff (see the BEA Web site, referenced above)—also leave out the value of nonmarket work. If I pay somebody to watch my kids, it shows up in GDP. I do it myself, it doesn't. It's an interesting example of how our measures of national wealth leave out "home production," creating a considerable bias against what economist Nancy Folbre calls "caring labor."

Do all these shortcomings mean that GDP doesn't paint an accurate picture of the economy? Yes and no. To the extent that you consider these omissions important and large—and I do—GDP as measured certainly doesn't give you an accurate *level* of economic activity. It overcounts our national wealth by failing to "net out" losses and environmental degradation. It undercounts by leaving out the value of caring labor. But, accepting its limits, GDP still provides us with the best available indicator of the *trend*—even with the aforementioned shortcomings, GDP reports reliably tell you whether and how fast the economy is growing. And since GDP growth has a profound impact on economic activities we care a lot about, like jobs and incomes, this is something we want to keep a close eye on.

That said, we should develop an alternative measure alongside the official one to account for the big omissions—most important, to account for bad environmental developments. Thanks to some enterprising, ethical scholars, the Green GDP movement has made some nice progress. Yes, it would be controversial, but our government statistical offices should give them a boost.[2]

Crunchpoint: Though GDP—the dollar value of our economy— leaves out some important stuff, it is still a useful measure of the size of the economy. In particular, we need to watch its trend—whether and how fast it's growing or shrinking—because much else flows from that: most important, jobs and incomes. When GDP growth slows below its trend, unemployment rises, which (a) isn't pretty and (b) raises our next question.

What is unemployment? And why does low unemployment seem to spook certain economic entities, like
the Federal Reserve and the stock market, so much?

To be unemployed, the way the officials describe it, is to be seeking work. If you're not looking for a job, even if you gave up because you couldn't find one, you're not counted as unemployed (such "discouraged workers" are not in the workforce).[3] Same if you're "underemployed," which is a disease I take up in the next question.

So that's the definition. How many people does it describe? For the year 2007, there were 7.1 million unemployed persons, generating a rate of 4.6 percent, which is actually pretty low in historical terms. The average over the 1990s was 5.6 percent; over the 1980s, it was 7.1 percent, due to some ugly high-unemployment years in the early '80s.

All of these numbers and rates raise the question, when is unemployment too high? Shouldn't we aspire to zero percent? Most of us want the lowest rate possible—there are those who would take exception to this sentiment, for reasons discussed in a moment—but zero is not realistic. There will always be at least "frictional" unemployment: people between jobs and those coming into the job market shopping around. Overall unemployment has never fallen below 2.5 percent, though the rate for college-educated workers is typically in that range or lower.

In fact, there's a big difference in unemployment rates by education level; in mid-2007, the rate for college grads was about 2 percent, while for high school dropouts it was about 7 percent. There are also large racial disparities; unemployment among African-Americans is typically about twice that of whites. Again, in mid-2007, unemployment for whites was 4 percent; for blacks, 8.4 percent. Part of this relates to the educational differences just noted, but discrimination plays a role here as well. That's one of the reasons we want to run as tight a labor market as we can: We want the demand for labor to be so strong that employers can't afford to discriminate. When the overall unemployment rate fell to 3.7 percent in April 2000, the rate for blacks fell to 7 percent, the lowest on record.

And this goal—very tight labor markets—runs us smack into the second part of the question.

Let me start by telling you about the Saturday paradox. On the first Friday of every month, the Bureau of Labor Statistics releases its report on unemployment and job growth in the prior month.[4]

The next day, the papers write about it, and herein lies the paradox. If it's a strong report, meaning solid job and wage growth with a tick down in the jobless rate, the "markets"—the stock exchanges, the bond traders—often get nervous. The reason: They're worried about an "overheated," or inflationary, economy, where a tight job market leads to higher wages, lower profit margins, and higher prices (faster inflation). The big worry by the investor class (and no, that doesn't include everybody—stock market wealth is highly concentrated) is that the Federal Reserve might raise interest rates and thereby slow the economy, which could cut into their racket.

So what we have here is basically a fundamental split between the aspirations of Wall Street and those of Main Street. Not that the suits on Wall Street want a recession, but neither do they want tight job markets forcing employers to bid up workers' pay. Like I said (see principle #2), economic relationships don't always play out like you'd expect, especially when there's real money on the table and the question is how is it going to be distributed.

To really get the dynamics at play here, you've got to understand the role of the Federal Reserve, a point I devote considerable space to in the next chapter. The critical point in this context is that about every six weeks, these wild and crazy Fed officials get together and do their best Goldilocks imitation, poring though bowls of economic data to decide whether the economy is too hot, too cold, or just right. And if they think it's too hot—if the unemployment rate looks too low to them—they'll hit the brakes (as explained later, they do this by raising the key interest rate under their control: the federal funds rate).

OK, but what's up with the Wall Street/Main Street split? The logic seems intact, but is it justified? Is this the best way to run a railroad?

I don't think so, for a number of reasons. First, many economists remain wedded to the idea that there is an unforgiving trade-off between unemployment and inflation. And it's not just that they worry that tighter job markets (lower unemployment) will kick inflation up a notch, like from 2 percent to 2.2 percent (in fact, there's pretty good evidence in support of that relationship). No, they fear that if unemployment goes low enough, inflation will spiral out of control, from 2 percent to 2.2 percent, 2.5 percent, 3 percent, and so on, until the Fed has to slam on the brakes and trigger a recession.

These fears should have been put to rest in the latter 1990s, when the tightest job markets in decades were accompanied by slower-growing prices, but this ideology goes back to Milton Friedman, and one unfortunate aspect of economics is that too often when the data contradict the theory, economists blame the data.[5]

A second reason for the split is a bit more prosaic: Unemployment and inflation are, in no small part, class-based concerns. Which is to say, when unemployment is too high, or job growth is too slow to keep up with the growing population, its costs fall largely on working families in the bottom half of the income scale. While very fast price growth of course hurts everyone, when inflation is ticking up, it's more painful to wealthy households with rich assets, or big financial market players worried about a Fed rate hike.[6]

Low unemployment has always been very important to low- and middle-income families, but it's a lot more so now. When the unemployment rate is too high—if we settle the trade-off in favor of those at the high end of the income scale—many workers will lack the bargaining power they need to claim their fair share of the growing economy. Remember, just because GDP is growing doesn't mean its benefits are broadly shared. In an economy with diminished union power, low minimum wages, and tough global competition, a truly tight job market (called "full employment" by economists) is the working person's best friend. History teaches us, quite unequivocally, that in its absence, growth is less equally distributed, and now more so than ever.[7]

There are a couple of themes here worthy of amplification in our national discussion of things economic. First, the stories told by these economic indicators—inflation, unemployment, GDP—are not as cut and dried as they might seem. Presidents will brag about GDP growth while ignoring the extent to which that growth is reaching the very people responsible for it. Newspaper stories will stress that an uptick in unemployment is a positive development since the Fed won't need to raise interest rates, without accounting for the problems caused by higher unemployment.

Second, it's easy and comforting to believe that the paths these indicators follow, like the paths of the celestial orbs, are outside of our control. You might support the ideas I've stressed regarding full employment, but getting there is outside of our control, right?

Wrong. Remember, economics is not a spectator sport, and the extent of unemployment is a legitimate concern for all of us. Tight labor markets are an essential antidote to the crunch, far too important to leave to a bunch of Wall Street suits and crusty central bankers.

Crunchpoint: The unemployment rate is the share of the workforce looking for a job—and this indicator has a lot of bearing on the extent of the crunch. It takes a truly tight job market—the kind of job market that gives workers some bargaining power (see principle #1)—to give most folks a shot at an equitable distribution of the fruits of their labor. The problem is, despite recent evidence to the contrary, some influential high-rollers in the stock market and at the Federal Reserve believe that low unemployment leads to an overheated economy with price pressures and squeezed profit margins. The other problem is that the folks on one side of this argument—the Fed—can actually do something about it, and in doing so, boost or undermine the efforts of working people. How about that? A seemingly straightforward indicator like the unemployment rate can provide considerable insight into whom key policy makers are pulling for or against.

■ **The rules I was taught**
  Fail to explain what I see.
  Perhaps they are wrong.

That's all very interesting, from 40,000 feet up. Here on the ground, I may not be jobless, but I certainly don't feel satisfactorily employed. Is there such a thing as underemployment?

Yes, there is, and it tends to run at close to twice that of the unemployment rate. In 2006, when the unemployment rate was 4.6 percent, the underemployment rate was 8.2 percent, which added 5.5 million to the ranks of the underutilized.[8]

This is an important and underappreciated question, because economists have a tendency to be quite absolute about certain concepts that are not always best understood in the context of such fine distinctions. A better way to conceive of the concept of unemployment is to think of what I'd call a "labor utilization continuum" (LUC). On one end of the continuum, your contribution to the economy through your job is at its full potential. You're working as many hours as you desire (this is important, because lots of part-timers like it that way), and your skills are fully utilized—that is, you're not a rocket scientist constructing "vente mocha lattes" unless that's the way you want it.

On the other end of the continuum, you're out of work. But the way we count it, only folks at that far end of the LUC are counted as unemployed, though they're surely not the only workers down on their LUC . . . (sorry). In fact, there exist a number of other categories counted by the Bureau of Labor Statistics (BLS) as underutilized, and a few more, counted by me.

The pie chart below documents millions of folks whose labor isn't being fully tapped. Data from 2006 show that after the seven million officially unemployed, the next-largest group is composed of over four million involuntary part-timers; they'd rather have full-time work but they can't find it. Since they're working, they're not counted among the unemployed, but that's probably not the way they see it. For the record, over 80 percent of part-timers are voluntary, so the underemployed are a minority. Still, there are a lot of them, and their numbers swell in times of weak job markets, though you won't see that swelling in the official jobless rate.

The other groups of underemployed persons, the so-called marginally attached, are neither working nor looking for work (it's the latter that keeps them out of the unemployment rate; if you're not seeking a job, you're not counted). The BLS judges them to be slightly, or marginally, attached to the job market, even though they're not looking. Some are "discouraged" workers: They gave up looking because they couldn't find work, gainful or otherwise. Others face a steep barrier between themselves and the job market, such as child care or transportation.

Then there's a group the BLS doesn't count, an admittedly hard group to identify: people who have jobs that don't fully tap their skills. Especially when the job market is not particularly tight, these folks show up in all kinds of places, from the coffee bar example noted above to the Russian engineer driving your cab. Economists used to look at this type of underutilization, and they found both high levels and an increasing trend. That is, by one measure, in 1990, 20 percent of the college-educated workforce held jobs that did not require their skill levels, up from about 12 percent in the mid-1960s: In our terms, they were underutilized.[9]

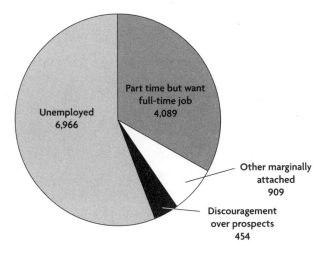

Figure 2.1. Underemployment in 2006, showing levels in thousands. (Source: U.S. Bureau of Labor Statistics.)

With about 42 million college grads at work in 2006, that implies over 8 million highly educated workers whose potential is not being tapped. The earlier research was criticized as not being precise enough, but my own updates, which use much better data, yield numbers that are only a few percentage points lower.[10]

And, of course, some underemployment doesn't apply solely to college grads. The decline of our manufacturing sector has led to lots of displaced skilled machinists out there who may not be college graduates but whose potential is far underutilized in the low end of the services. And then there are those who, due to racial discrimination or lack of exposure to quality education, never even had the chance to discover their labor market potential. In what is a true human tragedy, their talents, never tapped or developed, are lost forever.

Any way you cut it, there are millions more underemployed persons, even in good times, than you'd know from the official measure. Such underutilization is a problem for them (less labor market income and thus lower living standards than they'd prefer), as it is a problem for us (they could and should be contributing more to output). I discuss one important way to push back against this problem in Chapter 5: Economic officials must take the necessary steps to ensure a full-employment job market. Robust job creation is the enemy of underemployment.

Crunchpoint: Unemployment as currently measured is actually a pretty extreme location on a much wider continuum, a wide range of conditions that run from working like a hamster on a treadmill to being a complete couch potato. Between these extremes, there are millions more workers, or potential workers, whose labor is underutilized in one way or another. Being underemployed—as the questioner has recognized— hurts their economic prospects and undermines our economy's potential.

Economists and business reporters seem to go gaga over productivity growth. Why is it such a big deal?

An economist lands on a distant planet. He is greeted by alien emissaries. Anxious to learn about the planet, the economist questions the aliens. But instead of the classic "Take me to your leader," he inquires, "What is your trend productivity growth rate?" (This scares the aliens and they zap him into dust.)

When economists talk about productivity growth, we get a faraway look in our eyes, and you can almost hear a choir sing a solemn chord on high. That's because productivity growth, or output per hour worked, is a measure of efficiency, and economists love efficiency.

Let me explain. Suppose we have a little doughnut factory (mmm . . . doughnuts . . . mustn't write when hungry . . . mustn't go downstairs for doughnut . . . mustn't buy doughnuts on days when working at home . . . must concentrate . . . doughnuts kill productivity . . . and, we're back!), and we make 100 doughnuts per hour. Next week, with the same number of workers, we make 110 doughnuts per hour. Our productivity just went up 10 percent because we're making 10 percent more doughnuts with the same "labor inputs" that used to make only 100. (Note clever substitution of "labor inputs" for hours worked—now you too can go on TV and sound obscure and annoying.)

You may wonder, how could that happen? What fairy dust enabled our staff to kick up its doughnut production by 10 percent? It could be capital investment, as in they bought a new, improved doughnut maker; it could be that they reorganized the way they work; or it could be a tough new boss squeezing more doughnuts out of the production staff.[11]

However it materialized, the reason why productivity growth is so important is that it's a primary determinant of living standards. Greater efficiencies create more opportunities. The availability of more doughnuts may not help much, outside of creating more work for heart surgeons. To take a positive real-world example, we've been tremendously efficient at manufacturing computers, and now computers are cheap and available to those whose low incomes used to preclude them from owning such stuff.

So, the main way society advances its living standards is through more efficiently providing the goods and services that people want and need. It doesn't mean that folks will necessarily own more stuff, though that's certainly how it's played out here in America, a country where, after one of the most devastating attacks on our homeland in our history, our president advised us to get out to the malls and "down to Disney World." [12]

In France, on the other hand, they take their higher productivity growth in more time off. In fact, consumption makes up about 70 percent of U.S. GDP (a variable of which you now have intimate knowledge), compared with about 55 percent in France.

And that's the beauty of productivity growth. If productivity grows 2.5 percent (about the underlying annual growth rate in the United States since 2000), that means we can either have 2.5 percent more stuff for each hour we work, or the same amount of stuff with fewer hours worked.

Therefore, faster productivity growth is pretty much an unequivocally good thing. But there is a catch—a distributional one—and it's really important. Here, a picture is worth many words.

Because of the link between productivity and living standards, the mantra among economists is, "As rises productivity, so rise the fortunes of working families." We generally assume that productivity is a rising tide that lifts all boats.

Now, take a look at the graph. What you see there are productivity and the real income of the median family, the one smack in the middle of the income scale—half have higher incomes and half have lower. For years, productivity and median family income grew in lockstep. It's easy to see where people got the impression that if you played by the rules, the benefits of higher productivity would be yours to enjoy. [13]

Whatever blew a hole in that relationship? In a word: inequality. Starting in the latter 1970s, growth started to become more concentrated among higher-income families. There are lots of reasons—it's more *Murder on the Orient Express* (a mystery movie where there turned out to be

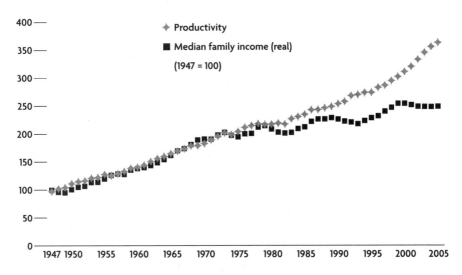

Figure 2.2. Growing together, growing apart: productivity and real median family income, 1947 to 2005. (Sources: Productivity, nonfarm business: U.S. Bureau of Labor Statistics; family income: U.S. Census Bureau.)

multiple "perps") than one smoking gun. But we can no longer assume that workers will get their fair share of the growing pie, even if its growth reflects their contributions.

That's why they call it inequality: It's not equitable. You help to create a more productive economy, but a disproportionate share of the gains flows to someone else.

Crunchpoint: There's good reason to celebrate faster productivity growth—without it there would not even be the potential for higher living standards. But in one of the most important and fundamental economic changes over the past few decades, we can no longer assume this potential will be realized. When it is not, the living standards of many working families fail to keep up with overall economic growth.

■ **My work, my value added**
Is growing the pie . . .
Slice, please.

Why do economists seem to fear inflation? And why do prices always go up, never down?

It's true. Today's economists worry most about price growth, otherwise known as inflation.

And we've got some good reasons:

- Higher prices mean less buying power—that is, lower "real" incomes ("real" meaning adjusted for inflation), and less real income means less consumption, investment, and growth.

- We know the Federal Reserve worries about that scenario, so we worry that if inflation grows too fast, they'll hit the brakes, as it were, raising interest rates to slow down the economy and lower the rate of price growth.

- We worry that once high inflation is in the system, it can be tough to squeeze out.

Why do prices always go up? Now, don't throw the book across the room, but they don't. Believe me, I know all about that last trip to the supermarket and stop for gas on the way home. As stressed earlier, a lot of highly visible prices have been rising quickly, a lot faster than average. But some other prices have been rising more slowly or even falling.

As I noted in answering the question from the overworked San Franciscan in Chapter 1, the biggest price declines have been in computers and electronics. Thanks to globalization and technological advances in IT, you can get scads more computer power now for a lot less bucks than a decade ago. The question is, when you get home from your third shift of your second job, will you be up to surfin' the Net?

Admittedly, these isolated cases of falling prices are exceptions, and most prices rise most of the time. The reason usually has to do with either economic fundamentals or some seller taking advantage of pricing power. The fundamentals are supply and demand, and a shortage of the former or a spike of the latter will nudge prices up. Most workers expect and get some increase in pay over time, such as a yearly COLA (cost of living adjustment), and firms may try to pass these wage increases along in higher prices.

A particularly interesting determinant of the rate of inflation is . . . the rate of inflation. Or, more precisely, the rate that people have come to expect. If we expect prices to rise and keep rising, then when they do so, maybe because of a supply shortage or because producers start flexing their pricing muscles, we don't go on strike in protest and stop buying stuff. We accommodate the increase, and that signals the price setters that we can live with faster inflation. If, on the other hand, our inflation expectations are "well anchored" (firmly locked in our thinking), we will respond to price hikes with some disdain, signaling producers that if they want to see our wallets, they'd better revert back to the slower price growth regime.

It may sound like far-fetched wishful thinking—"You can have whatever rate of inflation you desire, if you want it bad enough"—but inflation watchers obsess about the public's inflationary expectations. The Federal Reserve in particular puts great stock in this and will work very hard to convince economic actors—which is to say, people—that it will do what it takes to keep inflation well anchored, Matey.[14]

The tautness of the job market plays a key role here, too. Economists recognize a trade-off between unemployment and inflation—when the former is very low, the latter runs higher. Tight job markets give workers greater bargaining power, as employers need to bid compensation up in such climates to get and keep the workers they need. Once again, if such employers hope to keep their profit margins intact, they'll try to pass these prices forward to consumers.

In fact, this feared scenario—oh no . . . workers are getting raises . . . somebody do something!—lies behind the economists' biggest inflationary nightmare: the wage/price spiral. It's a tight job market, so workers get a raise. Firms pass the wage increase on to consumers, but lo and behold, workers also buy stuff, and when they discover that higher prices are eating up their fatter paycheck, they push for another raise. And the spiral is, allegedly, under way.

The thing is, for decades now, this has been nothing more than a scary campfire story at the economists' weenie roast. In a global economy, and one in which less than 10 percent of our private sector workforce is covered by a union contract, workers don't have the clout to keep pushing for raises. For that matter—and again, it's a function of increased global competition—most firms don't have the pricing power they used to. In fact, the last time we saw truly tight labor markets—the latter 1990s—unemployment fell to its lowest level in 30 years (4 percent in 2000), and, true to the full-employment/bargaining power story, wages rose at a faster clip than they had in years. But, and here's the kicker, inflation *de*celerated—its growth rate actually slowed. So while the spiral scenario may still haunt economists, it's a phantom menace, not a real one.

In fact, I remember when we used to worry more about unemployment being too high than too low. Lemme jest take off this ol' wooden leg here and tell y'all about the old days, when we fretted more over getting to full employment than whether inflation was in the Fed's "comfort zone"—low enough that they didn't see the need to raise interest rates. Despite the recent historical record, all that wage/price spiral stuff still has economists spooked, so we'll probably keep hearing more about price anxiety than job anxiety.

And yes, there's a class bias in here. Full employment is most helpful to the least advantaged, while inflation erodes the value of assets held by the rich and powerful, and they don't like that.[15]

Crunchpoint: Economists fear inflation because it lowers the buying power of any given income level and leads the Fed to raise interest rates that slow the economy's growth. However, there's a strong case to be made that global forces and weaker worker bargaining power have weakened inflationary links in ways economists do not yet appreciate. While nobody likes fast price growth, we should worry a bit less about inflation and a lot more about getting to full employment. Because although prices actually drop in some categories (like consumer electronics), that's small consolation when worker pay doesn't keep pace with rising prices for the basic necessities.

What is a recession and why do they occur?

When you lose your job, it's a shame. When I lose mine, it's a recession.

Like waves in the ocean, though less soothing to look at, our economy runs in fairly regular cycles, gradually rising from the trough, then hitting a peak before slowing again. The low point—the trough in the wave (less artful description below)—is the recession.

But economies aren't natural phenomena—why should they have cycles?

I've never seen a good answer to that, and one reason is that, thankfully, there haven't been so many recessions that a clear pattern emerges. Moreover, some underlying economic dynamics have been changing lately, and the causes, frequency, and nature of recessions may be changing as well.

Technically, as stated by the group of economists who make the call—the National Bureau of Research Business Cycle Dating Committee (sounds like a support group for guys who can't get dates through normal channels)—"A recession is a significant decline in economic activity spread across the economy, lasting more than a few months, normally visible in real GDP, real income [that is, income adjusted for inflation], employment, industrial production, and wholesale-retail sales." [16] "Visible in real GDP" has informally evolved to mean two quarters wherein GDP contracts, as in the economy actually shrinks.

Once a recession is over, the growth period following it is called a *recovery* or an *expansion*, and recession + recovery = business cycle. For example, the 1990s business cycle includes the recession of 1990–91 and the expansion from 1991 to 2000. A little makeup and you're ready for your own cable show.

That's the what. Here's the why: Recessions result from some shock to the economic system. As of this writing, the last recession hit in March 2001 and was the result of the bursting of speculative bubbles in financial markets and IT (information technology) investment. Investment is a key component of GDP, and when it headed south in late 2000, it triggered a recession that was quite mild in GDP terms, though acutely felt on the jobs side. Once we got that recession out of our system, a housing bubble inflated and then burst circa 2007, and this too put a hurtin' on the economy. (What's a bubble and how do they come to pass? That's next.)

In fact, the impact of the bursting housing bubble, occurring as I write these words, provides a useful, albeit unfortunate, case study. As of early 2008, an official recession has not been called, but many economists, myself included, believe we're in or near a downturn (the cautious officials make the call after the fact).

As housing prices rose in the 2000s—and as I describe next, speculation played a big role here, just like it always does in a bubble—lots of homeowners became wealthier. After all, for most of us, our house is our biggest asset. That wealth filtered through the economy, as folks refinanced their mortgages based on the new, higher price, and then borrowed against their homes. It may sound like a fairly obscure source of economic stimulus but it wasn't. We're talking literally hundreds of billions of extra bucks flowing through the system.

Well, I got one word for what happened next: pop! Gravity has a nasty way of reasserting itself, and in mid-2007, home prices started falling back to earth with a vengeance. The direct impact of the meltdown have been (a) hundreds of thousands of foreclosures—that's when homeowners default on their mortgage debt—mostly among those whose low credit ratings put the in the sub-prime end of the housing market, and, (b) much more broadly, falling home prices.

Those fallouts, by themselves, would not necessarily lead to a recession. But the damage to the economy goes much deeper, and it's a good example of how problems can travel the economy's circulatory system in a way that ultimately lays the patient low. The housing bubble was inflated by all kinds of creative and innovative—these are the nice words for them—lending schemes. The loan-rating agencies and bank regulators, including the Federal Reserve, were asleep at the switch, and many of these shaky loans worked their way into the financial system, both here and abroad. This led to a freeze in credit markets, and this economy thrives on free-flowing credit.

Also, as home prices fell, homeowners were much less prone to refinance their mortgages and pump some of that new found cash into the economy. Absent economic stimulus from the housing sector, we counted on the job market to provide consumers with the income they need to keep the economy moving forward (remember, consumption is 70 percent of GDP). But with related job losses in residential construction, financial markets, real estate, and so on, the job machine stalled in late 2007. Consumption stumbled next, and, again, though this was not made official as of early 2008, it was probably the last gasp for the 2000 business cycle.

Other recessions, such as those back in the 1970s, resulted from the increase in the price of oil. When the price of an important economic input like oil rises, both production and consumption are strained, and the economic results can get pretty ugly. The goodish news is that despite our "dependence on foreign oil," as the phrase goes, the overall economy is less susceptible these days to price shocks from oil. This is partly because our manufacturing sector has shrunk—energy is a much bigger input in manufacturing than in services—and partly because we use energy more efficiently than we used to, though, yes, we'll need to do a lot better here.[17]

The biggest recession in modern times was, of course, the Great Depression, a deep economic contraction lasting not months but years, with tremendous and tragic human costs. That was also partly the result of speculation, but the problem was greatly exacerbated by economic officials who assumed the market would self-correct (it's worse—they erected trade barriers and raised taxes, while the Federal Reserve, whose most important job is to offset such shocks, watched from the sidelines).

We are less likely to make those same mistakes now. Instead, we make new ones: we've got a bubble problem, and economists are only now beginning to recognize the damage caused by these bubbles. But the Federal Reserve has become more effective at steering through the

How Can a Recovery Be Jobless?

An economic recovery without jobs? Sounds like a day without sunshine, a birthday party without a cake, a bagel without the cream cheese. But the last two economic expansions—the ones that started in the beginning of the 1990s and the 2000s—both began with many months of an economy firing on all the key cylinders except one: job growth.

What happened?

The challenge in answering that question is that we have only two cases to analyze, so file the following explanations under what lawyers call "probable cause."

Small Dip, Weak Bounce

As ye have fallen, so shall ye rise. Historically, the economy has contracted fairly severely over recessions. During the 1970s and 1980s downturns, GDP fell around 3 percent. In the early-1990s recession, the decline was 1 percent, and in the 2000s, about zero. Like I said, thanks to globalization and a vigilant Federal Reserve, recessions are both rarer and milder. That's good, of course.

But how does this play out in the job market? That, it turns out, has not been so good.

When the economy tanks, lots of people stop consuming and investing. Next, labor demand, which is derived from those very activities (consuming and investing), tanks too, and workers get laid off. At that point, something interesting and important happens: Demand starts to get pent up. Because their cash flow is temporarily disabled, folks put off those big- and even little-ticket purchases.

Thus, you get a bit of a pressure-cooker effect: When the downturn ends and growth starts to percolate, that pent-up demand is let loose, and you get a nice bounce back, in both GDP growth and jobs. The growth norm for the year after a recession ended used to be 6 to 8 percent. In the 1990s it was 3 percent; in the 2000s, 2 percent.

That's just not enough oomph to get the job (creation) done.

Thanks to the aforementioned forces, we now appear to get a break from the pain of deep recessions. The downside is that we don't get much of a party when they're over.

Just-in-Time Inventory . . . for Workers

Another big change stems from the evolution of employers' cyclical hiring practices—changes in how firms approach staffing and the business cycle.

The old model of recessions in the workplace was pretty simple. You'd get a hiccup in growth, a bunch of factory workers would get furloughed, they'd trudge off home for a few months, and then they'd get called back to the factory once the downturn was played out.

Over the last few decades, in part due to the shift to less-stable service sector employment, employers have gotten much better at calibrating the size of their workforce to meet the spikes and dips in demand. Technological advances and globalization have allowed firms to turn on a dime when it comes to stocking their inventory, beefing it up quickly in fat times and cutting it back in lean ones. Well, they're apparently able to do that more and more with their workers as well these days, reacting to changes in demand by staffing up and down with much more precision than used to be the case.[18] Some firms, like Microsoft, have embedded this practice in the structure of their workforce by having a peripheral group of temp workers around a hub of core workers.[19]

One way to document this shift is to note that after both the 1970s and 1980s recessions, the percentage of workers who were involuntary part-timers (the unhappy folks who work part-time but want a full-time job with more hours, better pay, and fringe benefits) fell by about a point as a share of the workforce. After the 1990s and 2000s recessions, this just-in-time inventory indicator didn't fall at all; in the 2000s case, it ticked up a bit.[20]

This change is showing up in three ways in the new economy. First, we have the jobless recovery, a not-so-pleasant development. Second, we have observed faster productivity growth than would otherwise be the case, as firms can cut hours to match falling output more quickly than they used to. Finally, and this is the crunchy part: There's less employment security. Widgets and their families experience little downside from just-in-time inventory practices . . . workers and their families take it much harder.

shoals of economic shocks, and there are more automatic stabilizers, from safety nets to progressive income taxes (so your tax liability falls with your income, partially offsetting the blow), that help to keep the economic bicycle from teetering over when it slows. None of this implies the demise of the business cycle—a fine predictor of recessions is when economists say, "We've conquered the business cycle." It's just that there's some reason to believe/hope we've gotten better at avoiding deep recessions.

But before you threaten to revoke my "dismal scientist" card, let me note a troubling feature of the last two recessions. Well, really it was the last two recoveries: They started out "jobless." That is, in both the early 1990s and 2000s, the recession daters declared the recession over, yet we kept losing jobs for many months.

But didn't I say that employment growth was one of the things the recession daters look at when ringing the "Recession's over" bell? Yes, but it's just one of numerous indicators, and apparently they're downplaying its significance. What's more, there's a class bias embedded in this weighting scheme. As I've stressed throughout, we all love GDP and industrial production, but given that it's jobs that fill the wallet, these jobless recoveries can really take a toll on those least able to blithely ride out the recession: working- and middle-class families that depend on their paychecks, not their global portfolios. In fact, it took us almost four years to regain the jobs lost over the last recession/jobless recovery, more than twice the historical average.

It's one of the reasons why recoveries don't feel as good as they used to, and it's part of the next discussion.

Crunchpoint: Recessions are occasional economic contractions that result from some shock to the system. Thanks in part to better macro-management, they appear to be getting shorter and further apart. But the last two recoveries have started with a long period of joblessness, so for many working families, each recovery felt more like a recession than it should have.

Seems like we're forever blowing bubbles. What is an economic bubble, why are they bad, and can they be avoided?

The recession discussion highlighted the damaging role of speculative bubbles in our economy.

An economic bubble occurs when the price of something goes up well beyond what we would expect given the underlying fundamentals of supply and demand. If the jelly bean crop is destroyed by a sudden frost, we expect their price to rise. Or if suddenly everyone wants an iPod and the supply is fixed, their price will likewise go up. These are not bubbles yet—they're standard price increases based on real changes in supply and demand.

But sometimes prices rise quickly because a growing number of investors believe that the value of a particular asset, from a tulip bulb to fiber-optic cable to houses, is going to grow quickly and keep growing. They may not want the asset themselves—during the recent housing bubble, people bought homes not to live in, but because they thought they could "flip" them (buy low, sell high)—so it's not really demand driven in the iPod sense.

In fact, what's important to bubble investors is not the real, underlying economic need for whatever investment is driving the bubble. The bubble investor cares about one thing: Do other people still believe the price will keep rising? It might be obvious to as-yet-undiscovered aboriginal tribes that investing in firms with no products or profits is rarely a good idea. But if enough people with enough money believe that enough other people think such investments are the cat's meow, watch out: It's bubble time. (That phrase "enough people" is important. There will always be some folks engaged in random speculation. It takes a crowd to inflate a bubble.)

What's so bad about that? Well, for one, as we saw in late 2000, when bubbles burst, they can trigger recessions. But there is a less obvious fallout: Bubbles take a long time to mop up, and they have a lasting negative effect on economic activity.

Don't Know Much About GDP

If I asked you to name some growth industries in the new economy, "telecom" would probably be on your list, and rightfully so, given advances we've made in that area. But during the IT/dot-com bubble of the latter 1990s, deregulation of communications markets drove billions of dollars of speculative overinvestment in fiber-optic cable. Employment in telecom shot up about 40 percent, peaking in March 2001, the same month the recession began. Six years later, telecom jobs are down 30 percent; if you thought this was a growth sector—and these are good jobs, by the way—think again. The bubble severely injured it, and not just for a few months, but for years.

You could argue that we're just back to where we're supposed to be, but that's sugarcoating. The bad thing about bubbles is that, just as the herd gets whipped up into a speculative frenzy—former Federal Reserve Chairman Alan Greenspan called it "irrational exuberance"—so do they get clinically depressed post-bursting. Investors, who maintain a key position in the economic drivetrain, get irrationally cautious, and that's one reason why we suffered the longest jobless recovery in our history coming out of the 2001 recession.

Should bubbles be avoided? Can they be?

It's my impression that economists and policymakers have not quite recognized just how damaging these bubbles are—how lasting their damage is, in the sense just discussed. And just as the effects of the IT bubble were wearing off after years of retrenchment in that critically important sector, the housing bubble inflated. By mid-2007, that too was deflating. As we just discussed in our "anatomy of a recession" section, the deflation of the real estate bubble has so far sliced numerous percentage points, amounting to hundreds of billions of dollars, off of real GDP growth. As many as two million people may lose their homes to foreclosure, and credit markets have frozen as investor sentiment whipsaws from ebullient to emulsified.

There are at least two ways to keep bubbles from inflating: jawboning by people with very influential jaws, and regulation.

The jaws I'm thinking about here belong to the chair of the Federal Reserve. Others, like the secretary of the Treasury, might help, too, but there's no economist with greater clout than the Fed chair. And, as noted earlier, Alan Greenspan, who held the post as the dot-com bubble inflated, made a run at the bubble with his "irrational exuberance" comments. But he quickly dropped the language; and when pressed, he basically took a "Bubble? What bubble?" stance thereafter.

Later, when we folks asked why he gave up, Greenspan argued that the Fed has neither the ability to recognize bubbles nor the tools to deflate them. The first part of that argument is simply not credible: The chief himself recognized the irrational nature of the stock market's climb in the latter 1990s. Regarding the lack of tools, he argued that "it was far from obvious [that the bubble] could be preempted short of the central bank inducing a substantial contraction in economic activity, the very outcome we were seeking to avoid."[21]

Well, we got the contraction anyway—and believe me, financial players hang on every word that the Fed chair utters. He could have talked the bubble down somewhat, and he should have.

The other option is regulation, and that's always a lot stickier. You want to set rules that restrain obviously bad stuff but don't kill the creative energy that's inherent in markets. But if done with the right touch, it can work.

And there is some low-hanging fruit here. If people want to make crazy investments in profitless companies, we should let them. But what about when profitless firms pretend they're doing great and cook the books accordingly? Deregulation during the 1980s and 1990s of banking and accounting standards contributed to this fraudulent behavior, and that helped to blow up the market bubbles. Since then, Congress passed rules to block such behaviors—through the Sarbanes-Oxley Act—but they are continuously under attack by corporate forces with short memories.

As the housing bubble started to deflate in 2007, we began to learn about some more low-hanging regulatory fruit that we would be wise to pick. Unscrupulous mortgage lenders lent all kinds of money to people who quickly got in way over their heads. Insiders in the industry called these "liar loans" because the loan agent often inflated borrowers' earnings so that they would qualify. There were "prepayment penalties" (a penalty for paying off your mortgage early, to keep you paying interest as long as possible), interest-only loans (no down payment), and mortgages that started out nice and low, only to reset quickly (often within two years) to levels clearly beyond the means of the borrower. Not that borrowers were always innocent bystanders—it takes recklessness on both sides of the deal to inflate a bubble.

Such shell games are custom-made bubble machines. Regulating these practices—not prohibiting them (well, "liar loans" have to go), but restricting their use to keep vulnerable players out of that particular casino[22]—is a no-brainer, but the political power of the deregulatory crowd over the past few decades has often trumped reasoned lending policies (see principle #1).

We also might want to consider ending the tax advantage for people buying expensive second homes. When the stock market bubble burst, some investors went over to real estate, and since you can deduct the interest payments on up to a million bucks of mortgage debt on your first *or second* home, our tax code creates a tax incentive to speculate. There was a time when incentivizing home ownership across the income scale made a lot of sense, but that time is over. We should consider ending or reducing the deduction on second homes.

How about this bumper sticker? "Houses: Nobody gets two until everybody has one."

Crunchpoint: An economic bubble occurs when speculation raises prices well above what supply and demand would dictate. Economists, given our default position of deep admiration for market forces, have been slow to recognize both the formation and lasting damage done by bubbles. We should learn from past mistakes and start taking action— like identifying them sooner and discouraging the speculative investment on which they feed— to deflate them before they form.

What is a "living wage" and how is it different from the minimum wage? Do either really help, or are they just a good way for well-meaning people to get slapped around by the invisible hand?

Bubbles, recessions, unemployment, the inequitable distribution of productivity growth . . . all of these play a role in the crunch many families experience today. But what can be done to ameliorate these economic pressures? In Chapter 5, I speak broadly about the anticrunch policy agenda, but a number of people asked whether so-called living wages, or wage mandates in general (rules prohibiting wage payments below a mandated level), are an important part of the solution.

These policies—the living wage is a localized phenomenon; the minimum wage is both a state and federal program—are popular among economic justice advocates and progressive politicians, and roundly hated by many in the business community, who would be obliged if we would just leave the setting of wages to them, thank you. Below, we go through the arguments on both sides.

These wage mandates are part of the solution—a small but important part. They certainly help low-wage workers, but the crunch for many in the middle class is beyond their reach. Their importance, however, goes well beyond the impact of the wage mandate.

In 1997, two very mainstream, highly respected economics professors, David Card and Alan B. Krueger, published a book called *Myth and Measurement* (Princeton University Press), wherein they presented a few years of careful research on the impact of minimum wage increases. As I discuss in greater detail below, econ textbooks treated the matter as "case closed." He who mandates wages is flying in the face of the invisible hand, and it shall smite him. Raise wages by fiat, the story went, and you'll throw a wrench in the economy with some very negative unintended consequences.

But Card and Krueger, using unique data and careful, elucidating statistical techniques, convincingly proved otherwise. The outcry against their work was predictable, but they changed some minds, and now even some of the textbooks are framing the issue more flexibly.[23]

But what struck me and a number of other renegades as significant was the chink in the armor of classical economics that their work exposed. If the textbooks were wrong about this, what other economic relationships and assumptions should go under the empirical microscope? It's a stark reminder of principle #2: Economic relationships often play out in surprising ways, contradicting both basic logic and textbook theory.

This is liberating stuff. We must think broadly and creatively about economic policy; the classical assumptions should never be ignored, but they must constantly be tested. They must be guideposts, not chains. The invisible hand is, well . . . invisible, and its discipline is not nearly as daunting as advertised by those who use it to keep all the goodies flowing their way. In short, we should, all of us, always be asking ourselves, "What kind of an economy do we want?" and trying new ideas, like living and minimum wages, to get us there. Believe me, for as long as we've had an economy, some very powerful people have been asking and answering that question. It's time we all joined the discussion.

Now let's get down to cases. What is a living wage, anyway?

It's a level of wages that must be paid to people in certain jobs in cities that have living wage ordinances, as mandated and set by local government. There are two basic flavors of living wage laws. One requires that firms under contract with the city must pay the living wage, and the other requires that firms receiving some type of subsidy or tax break must pay the wage.

About 140 cities in the nation have living wage laws, and the wage levels differ from place to place, ranging from around seven bucks an hour in Albuquerque, New Mexico, to the mid-teens in some California cities.[24]

Why would so many cities embrace this policy? Ask the advocates who did the heavy lifting (I assure you, not every city council goes gently into that good ordinance). In some cases, it's about trying to preserve the quality of public sector jobs that have been outsourced.

In my old hometown, for example, the town government outsourced the garbage collection to a private sector firm to save some money. It even sold them the town's garbage trucks—which, by the way, stopped coming up your driveway so you now had to take the garbage down to the end of the driveway. No biggie—I'm just saying we got cheaper service, not better service (I'd moved away by the time this happened; they wouldn't have gotten away with this stuff if I'd still been there). Living wage laws serve to lessen the slide in pay for such jobs.

Another rationale is just good old antipoverty activism. The living wage coalitions seek something they call "economic justice"—there were no chapters on that in any econ textbooks I was ever assigned—and view the policy as a tool to raise earnings at the low end while building progressive coalitions.

OK, time to put on the economist's hat. That's right: Place the propeller beanie atop head, give the prop a spin or two, and . . . come up with reasons why you can't do stuff you think might help.

Won't raising wages by fiat lead to job losses? This is always a concern, whether we're talking living wage or minimum wage (the difference is that minimum wage covers everyone, not just those under city contracts). In fact, it's such a pervasive concern that it deserves its own Q&A in the sun. The evidence, which I've reviewed in mind-numbing detail, shows that job losses have not been a problem associated with the ordinances.[25]

For one, living wage ordinances tend to affect small numbers of people. Even in big cities, the number of workers that benefit from living wage rules is in the low thousands. Second, as noted in the next section, when wages rise by mandate, there are lots of other ways the increase can get absorbed. Some, typically a small share, of the costs of living wages get passed back to the city through higher contract costs, but the evidence mostly suggests that contractors suck it up in one way or another (lower profits and higher productivity, for example).

And remember, the higher-wage contractors tend not to feel any pinch from living wage laws because they're already paying higher wages. In other words, the ordinance blocks the low road.

So, are rules like these the answer to all that ails us? By no means. Living wage ordinances, by construction, reach too few to make a big dent in low-income work, but they do make a useful small dent.

But can you live on living wages? Not too well. The levels, as noted above, are not high enough to reliably pay for decent housing, quality child care, health care, and so on. It's important to recognize that these wage mandates are a balancing act. You can't tell low-wage employers to pay a wage that's high enough to meet the costs of these necessities, some of which, like health care, are driven up by our dysfunctional system. You can, and should, nudge them to get a little closer, though.

That's why we supplement low-income wages with a set of admirable policies called "work supports."[26] After much careful study (and I'm only half-kidding), experts have discovered that low-income working families need more money to make ends meet. The beauty part is that since they're working—they're playing by the rules, making a good-faith effort to lift themselves up—politicians from both sides of the aisle have deemed them worthy of extra help. So, along with living and minimum wages, we have, for example, the Earned Income Tax Credit, a wage subsidy to the tune of over $4,000 per year for a low-income working family with kids. We've got food stamps, and Medicaid, and SCHIP (the federal/state child health insurance program of publicly provided care for kids), and child care, housing, and transportation subsidies.

Don't get too excited—some of these are terribly underfunded and under frequent attack (child care, SCHIP). But while we have to accept that living wages may not be really living, we don't have to accept working poverty.

Crunchpoint: Living wages are local mandates ensuring that a small, select group of workers get a wage that's a few bucks above the minimum, and maybe some health coverage too. They're popular because they help scratch the itch of working poverty without generating the economic distortions their opponents worry about, but they're too low and reach too few people to make a big difference. Federal and state minimum wage laws reach many more workers, but they tend to be set at a lower level than living wages.

I vaguely remember my Econ 101 text asserting that government-imposed wage mandates force employers to lay people off. I must admit, it makes sense: Raise the price of something (workers), and people (employers) will buy less of it. Right?

Wrong, by principle #2 (economic outcomes cannot be assumed based on textbook relationships—they must be constantly tested, verified, and updated).

Get into a debate about passing a living wage somewhere or raising the state or federal minimum wage, and somebody's going to tell you that you only hurt the ones you love: If you raise wages by fiat instead of waiting for the market to get around to it, employers will have to lay off workers who are, because of the mandated wage hike, too expensive.

Sounds plausible, but here's the rub: It's been largely decided and argued on theoretical grounds, but it's an empirical question. You simply can't trust the assumptions.

Most people are quick to accept that higher prices lead to lower demand. You raise the price of Snickers, I'll buy M&M's instead. So it is that economists—and, much more vocally, those who worry that a minimum wage increase will cut into their profits and who then hire the economists to do their shouting—argue that minimum or living wage mandates will do more harm than good.

But workers aren't candy bars. And there are lots of other ways for a wage increase to get absorbed into the system besides layoffs. There are the three Ps, for example: prices, profits, and productivity.

Ask yourself why the U.S. Chamber of Commerce and the National Restaurant Association lobby intensively against minimum wages (that is, follow the money).

Prices: The evidence is that some small fraction of the increase shows up in higher prices of low-wage-intensive goods, so you could see the price of a burger go up a touch. But it's never more than a few cents on the dollar, a change that hasn't been found to register much at all with consumers.

Profits: Is it purely out of concern for the employment status of low-wage workers, a group that, by the way, hugely supports such wage increases? No, the groups that represent low-wage employers spend lavishly on an army of lobbyists to stop anything that might raise their labor costs and cut into their profits. That's their job and they're good at it. When they lose, and workers win, one way in which the mandated wage increase gets absorbed is through lower profits.

Productivity: Paying workers more, especially moving their wage out of the sub-basement, leads to higher-quality work, fewer turnovers, and fewer vacancies, and these efficiency gains pay for at least part of the increase.[27]

For these reasons, minimum wage increases have not been found to lead to big job losses among affected workers. We know this because some high-quality research has tapped the natural experiments that come into focus when one state or city raises its wage and another state or city next door doesn't. This type of pseudo-experiment is as rare as it is revealing in economics, and it has helped us to go beyond the textbook models and predictions that have driven this debate for too long.

The results find somewhere between little and no effects from the higher-wage mandate. By "little," I mean that in no research I've seen, even in the most unfavorable to the policy, do you find any results coming anywhere close to finding that the policy is a net loser for affected workers. In other words, some very persuasive research on this finds no negative employment effects among affected workers, and some equally persuasive work finds small negative effects. But in every case, the benefits to low-wage workers far outweigh the costs.

Another reason you don't get big negatives here is that the political process precludes it. It would certainly be possible to set a living or minimum wage high enough to throw a wrench in the economy, but in all my experience—and I've been in the fray on this one for decades—the political horse-trading always seems to serve up an increase that is moderate at best. One side might start high and the other low (as in zero, or no increase) but the compromise tends to deliver a workable result.

Crunchpoint: Your old textbook got this one wrong, because the logic is too narrow. Research on minimum wage changes across the country shows that moderate increases—the only kind the system tends to serve up—do not lead to large numbers of layoffs among affected workers. In fact, any job-loss effects hover between very little and none: the cost of the wage increase is absorbed in other ways—including slightly higher prices, lower profits, and more efficient production—and low-wage workers gain significant and important benefits from the higher wages.

■ **We raise the minimum wage.
The low-wage worker
does a little better.**

3

Political Economy 202

Principle #1—and it's first for a reason—emphasizes the role of power in economic outcomes, a role that gets virtually no attention in formal economics training. Yet, as stressed throughout these pages, the power to steer economic goodies your way is at the heart of our most fundamental economic challenge: the growing gap between overall growth and most families' living standards. Imbalanced economic power is at the heart of the crunch.

In this country more than any other advanced economy, when you're talking about power, you're in spitting distance of politics. Thus, it's not enough to be an economist—to know the rules of economics. You've got to be a *political* economist: You must know how the rules of economics interact with the power structure of politics.

I'm not simply talking about lobbyists' tweaking legislation their way, or the congressperson who gets the "pork projects" for his or her district (that is, wasteful spending projects that line pockets back home), though of course that's no small part of understanding the intersection between politics and economic outcomes. I'm talking about political economics that goes on beneath the radar—which is where most of it takes place.

And what's going on is simply this: Critically placed persons are structuring government practices, policies, and philosophies to meet their economic agenda. What makes up that agenda depends on who's running the show. But for the past few decades—and note, this is not simply a George W. Bush critique—that's largely, though not always, been an agenda with two parts: (1) to unleash market forces from the alleged handcuffs of regulation, and (2) to redistribute wealth and power to those at the top of the wealth pyramid.

I wrote about this (d-)evolution in my last book, under the heading of YOYO economics.[1] That's an acronym for "You're on your own," and it embodies a political philosophy that got us in our current mess. Under YOYO economics, the sole plan to meet any economic challenge we face, from globalization to health care, is a tax cut, a private account, and a solid push off the plank into the deep and murky waters of competitive market forces, where "you're on your own" to sink or swim.

Operating in this mode leads its proponents to oppose worthy ideas that strengthen the diminished bargaining power of most working persons—ideas like minimum wages; a level playing field for those who would organize unions; a universal, nonmarket-driven approach to health care and pensions; progressive taxes; and less porous safety nets. Each of these ideas strikes at the heart of YOYOism, as they seek to pool the risks of economic insecurity over large groups of people, while unifying less advantaged groups under a WITT ("We're in this together") agenda.

The point is that a WITT agenda obviously leads to a very different political economy than does a YOYO agenda. In fact, the history of economic policy is nothing more than a ride up and down this continuum. As I write these words, the failure of YOYOism to meet the challenges of globalization, the growing health care crisis, not to mention category five hurricanes, has the YOYOs on the ropes. And presidential candidate Hillary Clinton, an avowed centrist, mind you, is explicitly critiquing YOYOs and articulating WITTicisms:[2]

> . . . the administration's theory about how we should manage our economy: leave it all up to the individual.
>
> That's why they want to privatize Social Security and let individuals bear the risks. It's why their answer to the health care crisis is limited to creating [a] health savings account, which allows the healthiest people to get the best deal, with little concern if the sickest get worse.
>
> They call it the ownership society. But it's really the "on your own" society. . . .
>
> It's time for a new beginning, for an end to government of the few, by the few, and for the few, time to reject the idea of an "on your own" society and to replace it with shared responsibility for shared prosperity. I prefer a "we're all in it together" society.

We may be poised—I'm confident that we are—to start moving down the continuum away from YOYO toward WITT. This cannot occur, however, if the YOYOs are dictating the terms of the debate. In what follows, I address some of their most common arguments and objections to a new political economics, one based on the WITT agenda. Needless to say, I find them wanting, which is a nice word for "lame."

s Social Security really going bust?

Most people think the answer is yes, and young people especially don't believe this government-sponsored pension system will be there for them when they retire. According to one recent poll, 72 percent of respondents did not believe Social Security would be around. For Gen Xers, born between 1965 and 1976, the comparable share was 83 percent.[3]

That's an incredible consensus, considering that it's wrong.

More precisely, it will be right only if we make the huge mistake of turning this consensus into a reality. This isn't an "If we only believe, we can make it so" moment, either. The program is elegantly structured, and with a few minor tweaks it will continue to deliver for decades to come.

First, what's so great about Social Security? Even to me, it sounds clunky and aged, like some old Buick waddling down the road spewing parts and smoke. But just because the program itself has long been eligible for retiree benefits doesn't imply anything. I mean, the Constitution is hundreds of years old, and everybody still likes that, right?[4]

Let's consider how it works. The sweat from the brows of today's workforce generates the wealth that helps to fund the economic security of those who came before us. (OK, I only break a sweat at the office when the AC goes down, but you get the point.) At the same time, when those of us at work today finally call it a day, we will leave behind an economy that is a lot more productive than when we found it.[5] The investments we made, in both human and physical capital, will help the next generation create yet more wealth. And yes, we will skim some of that wealth off the top—that is, we tax some of that income—for Social Security, as did our forebears.

A key point here is that Social Security solves an intergenerational problem—the natural dependence of those whose working years are behind them on the working-age population—with an intergenerational solution: the transfer of a portion of today's wealth to today's retirees.

So what's all the shootin' fer? Why does almost everybody think the program's days are numbered?

The answer is a combination of demographic change, Chicken Little alarmism, and a couple of potent negative forces: greed and antigovernment sentiment.

The demographic concerns come from the fact that our population is clearly getting older. The share of the total population that's 65 or older is expected to climb from about 12 percent in 2000 to 20 percent in 2030, raising the concern that we'll have too few workers supporting too many oldsters. But there are two problems with this argument.

First, the share of kids in the population will decline some, and this will free up resources to spend on older persons that would otherwise have been needed for kids. In fact, the "dependency ratio"—the share of kids and older persons to workers—is expected to stay within its historical range. Second, and of greater import, we may have fewer workers per dependents, but those workers will be a lot more productive. The actuaries who forecast such things for the Social Security program believe the nation's productive capacity will grow by 130 percent over the next 50 years, and that's actually a little pessimistic.[6] If productivity continues to grow at the rate that's prevailed since 1995, our output per an hour of work will be up 280 percent in 50 years. Either way, we will literally create a lot more wealth per hour worked. Together, we can count on these factors to defuse any alleged demographic time bomb.

The fact that there's no bomb in the room doesn't mean we can ignore the growing share of the elderly population. At some point down the road, we'll have to either raise more revenue or cut projected benefit payouts. These cuts are a bad idea, relatively easily avoided, but even with them, tomorrow's payouts will still be higher than today's. Today, we collect more in Social Security taxes than we pay in benefits. In about 10 years we'll have to tap those savings to make the needed payouts, and in about 40 years—again, with no changes—we'll have to raise taxes or cut benefits.

All of which brings us to the first point of departure from the conventional so-called wisdom that is handcuffing our nation—handcuffs we voluntarily, if unknowingly, put on ourselves.

When you read those words, "raise taxes or cut benefits," does your tummy clench up a bit? Do you unwittingly grimace, forced into a Hobson's choice by unforgiving fiscal arithmetic? Do you jerk your knee and shout, "No way!"?

If so, you're not alone. Just remember, that's the way they want you to feel. Who are "they"? Picture Mr. Burns from *The Simpsons* greedily tapping his fingers together. Actually, "they" are a small number (that is, small relative to the rest of us) of people who profit greatly from the widespread belief that any idea, program, or policy that requires public investment is bad. Dangerous. Un-American, unfair, unpatriotic. Spending, they say, will cripple the economy and turn us all into French socialists, nihilists, and existentialists.

Instead of accepting that dour assessment, when confronted with the choice to pay or cut, remember principle #3—tradeoffs happen, and they're not always benign—and remind yourself that there are some big questions to ask. Just how much money are we talking about? Where will it come from? What's sacrificed if we make the cuts? What's out there to take its place?

In some cases, like this one, I think you'll be surprised by the answers. According to the crack analysts at the invaluable Center on Budget and Policy Priorities, Social Security's shortfall through 2081, which is as far into the future as you'd want to predict anything, amounts to 0.7 percent of GDP.[7] Their table also answers question #2 above: It so happens the Bush tax cuts for the richest 1 percent of families come to—you guessed it—just about the same amount: 0.6 percent of GDP.

There's another way we can and should raise more money for Social Security: increase the salary cap on Social Security taxes. In 2007, earnings over $97,500 are not subject to the payroll taxes that support the program. Historically, around 10 percent of workers had earnings above the cap, but with all these runaway salaries, it's now more like 17 percent are flying above the radar.[8] We shouldn't let rising wage inequality deprive Social Security of needed funds.

The program's shortfall is simply not that big, and therefore it could be eliminated with some minor changes (and, just for the record, the Bush tax cuts are scheduled to expire—that's how they were sold to the public—so it would take no change at all to implement this part of the plan). You wanna talk big shortfall, you'll have to wait for the discussion about health care.

What's being preserved, and is it worth it? To my thinking, the intergenerational story I told above makes a lot of sense, and it is one reason why advanced economies have universal pension plans. But it's also the case that too few people save enough for retirement, and Social Security is one leg of the three-legged pension rocking chair (block that metaphor!), the other two being private pensions and savings. For many who are aging out of the workforce, these last two have been insufficient, which is one reason why we see people working quite a bit longer than they used to (not the only reason—greater longevity plays a role here, too).[9]

Finally, given that we need a universal pension system, is Social Security the best of all the alternatives? Surely there are other good ways to do this. Let's start with the darling of some conservatives: privatizing the program.

Whoops, I said "good" ways. It is generally agreed that replacing the current system with one that siphons funds from the current system to allow people to invest in stocks and bonds creates more problems than it solves. It does nothing to solve the shortfall issue. In fact, privatizing increases the shortfall and does away with the pension guarantee that's so integral to the success of the current plan.

But let it not be said that we who firmly reject private retirement accounts can learn nothing from the idea. In fact, we should invest some of our Social Security assets in stocks, to take advantage of their potentially higher returns compared with government bonds (the current system requires that assets from the program be invested in such bonds).

They do this in Canada by investing part of their Social Security trust fund in stocks, pooling resources instead of creating zillions of private accounts. In so doing, they manage to tap stock market returns without creating either the risk of individuals going bust or a bureaucratic nightmare. As some scholars who compared how different countries approach the pension challenge noted, "The Canadian experience shows that the cost of administering and regulating equity investments through a centrally managed trust fund is dramatically lower than through a myriad of individual accounts."[10] The concern is that you have the government owning a piece of private industry, and this creates worrisome incentives (like special contracts for favored firms . . . something that would never happen here . . . d'oh!). But such worrisome incentives could be handled by firewalls, as our northern neighbor uses.

Guess who rails against this idea? Many of the same investment firms that are cuckoo for private accounts. Why? Because it kills one of the main reasons for privatizing: millions of new accounts for them to administer. Can you imagine the business that would flow their way if even half the workforce opted for a new account to store a portion of their current payroll tax? Investment banks get hugely excited about this prospect, and they do not look favorably on losing those millions of accounts to big government.

Which brings us to the other group who wants you to believe that Social Security won't be there for you: the AGIs (antigovernment ideologues). To get where the AGIs are coming from, you simply have to recognize that Social Security is the biggest government program we've got, costing $600 billion in 2006 and comprising about a fifth of the budget. And while it's a universal program—everyone who pays in gets something out—it's progressive: Given what they contributed over their working lives, low-income workers get more out relative to their contributions than do high-income folks. Big and progressive . . . AGIs hate that.

Crunchpoint: Bob Dylan said, "Don't follow leaders, watch the parking meters." I'm not quite sure what that means, but I think in this case, it translates into: Don't let anyone tell you Social Security won't be there. With a few sensible, manageable changes, this venerable intergenerational contract can live on, a mutually supportive dance that's been linking the young and the old for generations.

Presidents are always going on about the economy, but do they really have much influence?

Yes, Virginia, presidents do matter when it comes to the economy—in fact, they matter a lot more than most economists like to admit.

It's de rigueur to dismiss all the usual presidential bluster on the economy as just that. And presidents do have a way of crowing about how their fingerprints are all over positive economic developments while nowhere near the scene of lousy economic outcomes. But modern presidents do have a major effect in a few key areas: fiscal stimulus, or giving the economy a jolt when it needs it; setting spending priorities; and good old power dynamics.

The first part, what is often called *Keynesian stimulus*, after the great economist who legitimized such actions, is less common, because, thankfully, we're not usually in recession (look back at Chapter 2, for a discussion of recessions, their causes, and their cures). When we are in a downturn, however, the mechanisms that keep the economy humming are jammed. For one reason or another, consumers aren't consuming, investors aren't investing, and employers aren't hiring. In such cases, presidents can work with Congress to stimulate the economy through a tax cut or even a "tax rebate" (lots of people get a check for a few hundred bucks), or through juiced-up government spending on one project or another.

President George W. Bush shoved a Keynesian tax cut through Congress in 2001, though with this guy there's always an angle. In the midst of a strong economy in 2000, he ran on a plan to cut taxes. But it wasn't until a recession was declared in 2001 that he used economic stimulus as a rationale. And, in fact, later Bush tax cuts that occurred outside of recession had other rationales. Recession? Tax cut. Recovery? Tax cut. War? Tax cut. Colts win the Super Bowl? Tax cut. When your only tool is a hammer, everything looks like a nail.

Certainly, presidents don't always go to the Keynesian place. If the recession looks shallow or short lived, it's going to be hard to get the stimulus into the system in time.[11] But it is one of their important tools.

The big story regarding presidents and the economy, however, lies elsewhere, deeply embedded in our power and trade-off principles (#'s 1 and 3). Specifically, where presidents flex their economic muscles is in the nuanced area of setting spending priorities and the resultant redistribution of power, resources, and opportunities.

Let me hit you with what I consider a pretty big number: $3 trillion. That's just about the size of the most recent U.S federal budget, and it amounts to about a fifth of the economy. How you spend that kind of money matters a great deal, and presidents have a lot to do with that. So don't let anyone ever tell you they don't influence economic outcomes. Of course, Congress plays a big role in shaping the budget, too, but the document originates from the executive branch, and the party that composes the first draft of the legislation always has the most sway.

To be shamefully, but usefully, reductionist, when setting spending priorities, presidents operate in three modes: redistributing, investing, and constraining.

When a-redistributing he or she goes, keep an eye on the president's target. Principle #3, trade-offs matter, is in play here. You can give tax cuts for people who don't need them, though they really do want them. You can funnel spending projects to your friends. No politician is blameless in this game, but just to take a pointed example from current events, let's look at the George W. Bush record.

One of the best outfits for crunching numbers on who benefits from tax cuts is the group Citizens for Tax Justice. Their name suggests an edge (though I don't think "Justice" implies a bias we should be worried about), but their reputation for purity in how they go about their analysis is stellar. In 2006, they took a look at who gained, and by how much, from the spate of Bush tax cuts that occurred over the president's first term, and this is what they found.[12]

The poorest group of families, those in the bottom fifth of the income scale (average income: $11,300), ended up with less than a hundred bucks from the cuts. Middle-income families, in the $40K range, ended up with about $700; and those at the top end, with an average income of about $1.5 million, well, they came away from the table with $52,000 in tax cuts.

Bill Clinton had a better record in this regard. In his first budget, for example, he raised taxes on the wealthy and greatly expanded the Earned Income Tax Credit (EITC). That's a wage subsidy for low-income workers, but it works as pure income redistribution through the income tax system. So this was kind of a Robin Hood moment, in terms of the president's redistribution mode.[13] But lest you think this stuff always follows a partisan pattern, note that President Reagan also championed a big boost in the EITC.

Investing some of that $3 trillion is another way presidents can affect the economy, often well down the road, by spending money on potentially productivity-enhancing projects that the private sector is unlikely to embrace. Al Gore may not have invented the Internet, but the government was the major player in getting it off the ground, and the productivity payback has been enormous. Moreover, the start-up costs and linkage needs of such an ambitious project put it outside the reach of the private sector. The same could be said of lots of medical and other scientific research.

But before you get too excited, or too incensed, depending on your orientation, keep in mind that federal investment in R&D amounts to about 1 percent of our economy. As I suggest later, while that may have been adequate in the past, it's not enough if we're going to get ahead of the environmental threats we face.

Constraining spending is another way in which presidents can influence the economy, for better and for worse. Generally, economists worry about the lack of spending restraint by presidents and other elected officials, and government spending has a pretty bad rep. But while presidents can hurt the economy by spending too freely, especially when they don't pay for it, the converse is also true. By neglecting productive investments or spending on services that people really want and need, like health care, it's possible to retard growth.

So how can we in the electorate recognize the right balance? What should we be listening for when presidents run their economy rap by us?

First, in an era when the market itself is generating huge inequalities, government should not exacerbate them. So when presidents go into distributional mode, watch out for Robin Hood in reverse. Someone who dropped in on our economic policy in the 2000s could be forgiven for thinking the big problem facing the American economy was that rich people didn't have enough money. I know all the mumbo-jumbo about cutting their taxes so they'll be more productive, but that supply-side nonsense has no credibility. In fact, as I've stressed throughout, the problem in today's economy is much less slow productivity growth than it is the distribution of that growth. So beware of upward redistribution.

I'll say more about public investment in Chapter 5. It's been very important in our past, and it will soon be so again.

Regarding spending restraint, economics is all about the best way to spend scarce resources, and when said resources come from you, me, and, if the spenders neglect to pay the bill, our children, restraint is a venerable goal in and of itself. That said, it's easy to overdo this one. Especially when it's "our money," we can easily resent its being spent. But before we jerk our knees in response to plans for government spending, we should look as closely as we can at what that spending is for. Is it for productive investments on behalf of future generations, or health care that's provided more efficiently than it is by the private sector (see the health care discussion in Chapter 1), or protection for our least advantaged citizens for stuff outside of their control, like, oh, I don't know, say, levees in poor neighborhoods?

Finally, presidents can throw their weight around in important ways that end up having an influence over how income gets distributed. When Bush acted by executive order to change the overtime rules in a way that favored employers over workers, this had obvious distributional consequences (even the generally pro-business Republican Congress tried to stop him, twice, but he didn't need their approval on this one). When Reagan fired the PATCO workers and Clinton opted to make NAFTA (a trade agreement that labor was against) his first big legislative priority, such actions sent important signals to markets about who was in and who was out. They tilted the balance of power, and power is at the heart of how economic outcomes get distributed.

Crunchpoint: Presidents have a great deal of influence on the economy. Those who take a balanced approach to the three tiers of spending priorities—redistribution, investing, and constraining—can make a big, positive difference in the economy and in the living standards of ourselves and our progeny. Those who play fair in the power game, keeping their thumbs either off the scales or moving back and forth from one side to the other, also provide important balance.

OK, so presidents wield some economic clout, but doesn't the real power lie with the Federal Reserve? Who are those folks, anyway? Is what they do that vitally important? And what part have they played in the crunch?

It's true: In some important ways, the chairperson of the Fed (short for Federal Reserve) is more powerful than the president on matters economic. Many times, I've heard the allegedly most powerful politicians in the country sound exactly like my five-year-old telling me, "Mom said I could!" except it's Greenspan or Bernanke in place of mommy (Alan Greenspan ran the Fed from 1987 to 2006, when Ben Bernanke took over).

Take, for example, the big tax cuts that George W. Bush implemented in 2001. Even though the government's accounts were in surplus at the time, Congress was wavering, worried about the impact of such deep cuts on our future ability to raise the revenue we need without adding to the debt. But when the Fed chairman at the time—Alan Greenspan—endorsed the cuts, their passage was assured. It turned out the "waverers" were right, but such is the clout of the nation's top economic official.

The top officials of the Federal Reserve, including the chairperson, are appointed by the president and approved by the Senate. While the Fed chair often confers with the administration and the Congress, there is a hands-off tradition regarding politics and the Fed (it was actually unusual for Greenspan to weigh in so directly on the tax cuts). The idea is that you don't want pols leaning on the Fed to tweak the economy their way at sensitive times, such as before an election. Some suspect the Fed does this for presidents, but I've not seen it.

The Federal Reserve System (there are twelve Fed banks throughout the country, with the headquarters in Washington, DC) is the regulator of the nation's banking system. The system was born in 1913, as legislators recognized that disruptive, destabilizing shocks to the economy could be avoided if there were a quasi-governmental system in place to pull some key policy levers at critical times. Bank panics, for example, in which investors and savers became deeply spooked by some development in the economy and withdrew all their money from the system, were not that uncommon back then, and the effects could be devastating.[14] The idea was that when such panics struck, the Fed could control the money supply and calm the markets.

You'll notice that 1913 is before 1929. The Fed blew it and failed to react to the huge market crash late that year, ensuring that the recession would deepen into the Depression. But since then, the Fed has generally been pretty effective at helping to stave off big market implosions. Even as I write this in late summer 2007, the Fed has been lending billions to banks throughout the country to offset a global contraction of credit caused by the sharp deterioration in the housing and mortgage markets.

This time, it's been a run not on banks, but on hedge funds and other esoteric institutions, but the theme is exactly the same. The herd is spooked, and what could be scarier than a stampede of institutional investors down Wall Street, designer ties flying behind them as they shred "collateralized loans"? We need the Fed to lower the red cape, stop the running of the bulls, and stabilize the markets.

Such runs, thankfully, are exceptional. Under normal conditions, the Fed's big job is to set the interest rate at which banks loan money, or *cash reserves*, to each other. (Hey, wake up! You asked the question. Excuse me if this part isn't a laugh-riot.)

This rate matters a lot, because it sets the cost of credit throughout the economy: Mortgages, bank loans, car loans—they all riff off of this *federal funds rate* (FFR). It's also the major tool by which the Fed tries to heat up or slow down the overall economy, and herein lies some serious controversy, as well as the answer to the question, why should I care about these deep nerds?

This little bitty number, the FFR, which for the last decade has bipped and bopped between 1 and 6 percent, plays a critical role in determining the pace of economic activity. I don't want to overdo the Fed's ability to set the pace: Especially in today's global economy, don't hold the image of evil (or benign) scientists tweaking a dial to set the level of economic activity precisely where they want it to be; but the Fed does, for example, play a determinant role as to where the unemployment rate stands.

In fact, according to congressional fiat, when the Fed isn't busy putting out economic fires, and it's usually not, its day job is supposed to be balancing inflationary pressures against the risk of weak growth, for which the FFR is its main tool. The analogy of hosting a party is often used, and it's a good one.

The officials of the Federal Reserve have invited us all over for a party—doesn't that make you feel a lot better about them?—and their job is to make sure we're fully occupied and having a great time, without overdoing it. They want us to be enjoying the finger foods, downing a glass of wine or two, perhaps even dancing a bit to their mellow orchestra (which reminds me: Alan Greenspan was a jazz saxophonist before turning to econ; I also used to play jazz, and once heard from someone who played with him that he wasn't half bad).

They don't want us guzzling booze, slam dancing to the Clash, and wrecking the property—that is, they don't want the economy growing too fast such that inflation begins to rise too quickly. So how do they keep the party polite? By raising and lowering the FFR, adjusting the cost of borrowing, and signaling the markets that they are satisfied with the pace of economic growth (leave the FFR unchanged), think it's too slow (cut it), or think it's too fast (raise it). In party terms, they can close the bar or roll out another keg.

That all sounds fine, except for one thing: It means we partygoers have to trust their judgment. Embedded in this model is the assumption that these unelected officials know precisely when the party's getting too hot or too cold. But what if they're wrong? What if you just got pumped up enough to hit on that amazing guy or gal you've been admiring since you arrived? You're strutting across the floor, the band goes into "Sex Machine," and just as you're about to make your move, Ben Bernanke kills the music, turns on the lights, and rips that rum and Coke from your hand. Talk about your buzz kill.

Shifting ever so slightly back to economic terms, if the Fed tightens precipitously—if it mistakenly raises the FFR when there's no real threat from inflationary pressures—its actions will unnecessarily lead to less job creation and higher unemployment. These developments will in turn diminish the bargaining power—there's that word again—of the millions of working families who depend on low unemployment to make sure they're getting their fair share of growth.

Moreover, there is a big distributional angle to the way this plays out. Different people in different income classes are affected differently by Fed moves. Those at the top end of the income scale have little to fear from a tick up in unemployment. They get their share—in recent years, much more than that—regardless. But those in the bottom half depend on full employment, a point I stress both throughout the book and in Chapter 5.

Let's turn again to a picture. The figure below plots the wage boost you get from one percentage point less unemployment for workers at different levels in the wage scale, from the lowest (10th percentile) to the highest (95th). If the bang for a decline in the jobless rate from, say, 6 percent to 5 percent were the same across the wage scale, you'd be looking at a

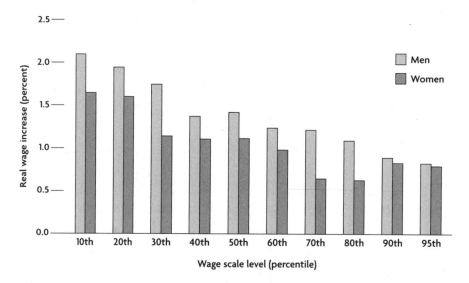

Figure 3.1. How much does a one-point decline in unemployment mean to earners at different wage levels? (Source: Jared Bernstein and Dean Baker, *The Benefits of Full Employment* [Economic Policy Institute, 2003].)

picket fence. Instead, you see a downward staircase. When unemployment ticks down a point, the real wage rises by 2 percent for low-wage men, but less than 1 percent for those at the top of the wage scale (and, in fact, the high-end wage results were statistically insignificant, meaning their response to lower unemployment is indistinguishable from no response at all).

So, when the Fed errs on the side of inflationary caution, they lay a hurtin' on those least able to absorb it. Some folks are going to have a great time at the party no matter when the Fed pulls the plug. Hell, they'll relocate to their yachts and keep it going all night. But most of us don't have that option; we depend on the Fed to get this right.

And for much of the past few decades, they've gotten this part of their job—not the rare crisis-intervention part, but the everyday setting-the-speed-limit part—more wrong than right. Not always, and the exceptions (most recently, the second half of the 1990s) are important, notable, and worthy of praise, but there is a bias at the Federal Reserve, and it has led the Fed to tilt against inflation, even when it is a phantom menace. For most of the past few decades, our labor market has not run at full employment, and that's one of the reasons why many people's living standards lag behind the overall economy.

Crunchpoint: It's a good thing we have a Federal Reserve to regulate the banking system and help stabilize the economy against disruptive shocks to the system. But the Fed also has a responsibility to use its powers to promote full employment, a condition that matters a great deal to low- and middle-wage workers. Thus, when the Fed fails to aggressively pursue this goal, as it has for most of the past few decades, broadly shared prosperity is much more elusive.

Should I care about the federal budget deficit? It seems big and scary, but what impact does it really have on the economy? Is it ever good to run a deficit?

Deficit . . . it sounds like a problem, as in "attention deficit disorder." I guess you could turn it around and be happy to have a deficit of misery, but that feels like a reach. A deficit sounds like not enough of something you wish you had more of. And federal budget deficits in the hundreds of billions, which have been the norm in recent years . . . well, that sounds like real money even by Washington standards.

What is it? In the case of the federal budget, a deficit is what you get when you spend more than you take in. You collect $100 in taxes and spend $110 in outlays, you've got a deficit of 10 bucks. Do that again next year, and now you've got a debt burden of $20. In economese, deficits are flows (like a river), and debts are stocks (like a pond), meaning every year you run a new deficit, your debt pile grows. The river of deficits flows into the pond of debts, so unless you reduce your debt, your water level rises.

Again, it doesn't sound good, right?

But here's the thing: Deficits in the federal budget don't have to be a problem—and in fact, if we're using the money wisely, they can provide an important source of current services and future growth. Where they become a problem is when (a) we waste the money, and (b) they get too big.

First, let's debunk the notion that any deficits or debt is de facto bad news. For lots of reasons, not the least of which is old-fashioned American thrift, some influential people hate budget deficits. Remember Ross Perot? He was the little dude who ran for president largely on "fiscal responsibility"—often code words for "I'm nervous about deficits, and you should be, too." Back then, a popular argument was, "You wouldn't run your family finances like that, would you?" Today, the Concord Coalition, an influential group of big shots, exists to wave the antideficit flag. The commonsense idea, then and now, is that families can't spend beyond their means, so why should the government be able to do so?

Except that many of us do just that, and for good reasons. We borrow to invest in college, an investment that typically pays for itself many times over. Or to buy something we need now rather than wait until we can finance the purchase without taking on any debt. If we're smart— and there's lots of not-smart borrowing, by people and their governments—we recognize that we'll have to pay principal and interest, and we're OK with that. In fact, if we invest wisely, and college is a good example, we'll be better equipped to pay back the loan.

Corporations do the same thing. They take on debt, usually through selling bonds, which are like IOUs that pay interest, in order to fund projects to generate future growth. Unless there is a good reason for it, investment analysts might look quite negatively at a firm whose debt-to-equity ratio is zero.[15]

Now, extend that to government and society. There are lots of cases where it makes sense for government to spend more than it is taking in. The classic example is Keynesian stimulus: boosting public spending or cutting taxes to offset weakness in the private sector. Productive deficit spending can also include investment in R&D, education, safety net programs, and other such *public goods*—things that society wants and needs but are insufficiently provided by the private sector.

Of course, like much in economics, not to mention life itself, the key to deficits is finding the sweet spot between healthy and excessive levels of borrowing.

Most economists are pretty hawkish about the deficit, meaning they're against it. The main reason is, they worry that the big gorilla in the room—the government—will gobble up all the savings in the room, leaving too little for the private sector. This gobbling, they fear, will push up interest rates—the cost of borrowing money—and depress productive investments in the private economy. They call this phenomenon *crowding out*, as Uncle Sam swaggers into the bank, elbows his way to the front of the line, and borrows all the capital in the vault, leaving nothing for the rest of us.

Not an unreasonable hypothesis, but recalling principle #3 from *crunch* economics, many of the simple, sensible, logical economic relationships don't always play out in the way you'd expect. What with all the moving parts—and in this case, with globalization hugely boosting the supply of capital available for borrowing—evidence for the crowding-out hypothesis is surprisingly elusive.

So, with moderate deficits, it's pretty unlikely that you'll see any upward pressure on interest rates associated with your mortgage, car loan, and so on. But what's moderate?

There's a little arithmetic involved, but basically, you want to keep the deficit flow down to the point where debt stock is growing no faster than the overall economy. That is, unless you've got a really good, temporary reason (like funding World War II), you don't want your debt-to-GDP ratio to grow.

So, if crowding out isn't usually such a big concern, are there other reasons to worry about budget deficits? In fact, there are a few big ones.

First, there's throwing good money after bad. In your world, borrowing for a home or college might be a great way to spend, but what about that bender in Vegas? Well, it may shock you to hear this, but government can throw money away, too. The last thing you want to see is borrowing to spend on some knucklehead's pet pork project.

Second, there's my personal favorite deficit problem: what economists call "structural deficits" (I like it because it's a simple criterion, like the rising debt-to-GDP ratio, for judging when you should get nervous about deficit spending). A structural deficit is what you get when you turn up the flow of deficits—and thus add more quickly to the stock of debt—at the same time as you cut taxes or ignore spending obligations coming down the pike. The implication of these deficits is that if something doesn't change, you—more accurately, your kids—won't be able to pay for the stuff you're promising without big, wrenching changes.

That may appeal to some nefarious "starve the beast" types, but believe me, it's asking for trouble. These are the folks who like the idea of crippling government debt because they believe it will ultimately bring the government to its knees. But that's an awfully cynical strategy. You want less government, fine. Tell us whose ox you're going to gore—which programs you're going to do away with—and we'll talk. But it is dishonest and irresponsible to borrow and spend without any consideration of how future generations will deal with the bill.

Which brings us to the last point: Since deficits ultimately have to be paid for by somebody, why should we ever shift the burden to future generations? Wouldn't it be better to just raise the needed revenue and take it from there?

Sometimes, as in the case of stimulating a weak economy, you don't have the time, but those are rare situations. Most deficit spending funds services or investments for which we simply haven't raised the money. And as Milton Friedman said, "To spend is to tax," meaning that any spending not paid for now must be paid for later by cutting somewhere else or raising new revenue.

But when Uncle Milty, renowned disparager of government, made that argument, he didn't mean it in a nice way, like I do. Fact is, as another great economist, Mick Jagger (he attended the London School of Economics—really!), said, you can't always get what you want. Meaning, in this case, that you can't always raise the bucks you need when you need them. And if the spending is worthwhile, you don't do current or future generations a favor by waiting.

Too often in today's debates, a politician will argue that $10 billion is better spent on deficit reduction than on meeting a pressing human need, when chances are, he or she hasn't thought it through at all. What if that deficit spending could help pay for quality child care for a working single mom who could finally get a foothold in the job market and start saving for her kid's college education?

Crunchpoint: Polonius's admonishment "Neither a borrower nor a lender be" might have been good advice for Laertes, but in public economics, it's OK to borrow. In fact, deficit spending is a fine thing if (a) we keep it down such that debt doesn't grow faster than GDP, and (b) we're using the money for stuff that society really needs. Tax cuts for rich people don't qualify; investment in Head Start does.

OK, so you say some deficit spending can be a fine thing. But I've heard nothing but negativity regarding budget deficits. Can you cite one other person, preferably of note, who can corroborate your story?

That's fair. I'm sure you've heard a lot of stormy rhetoric about the evils of deficit spending, and you may well be wondering whether anyone else shares these views I've been espousing. It's a good question and I'm not offended. Our modern urban centers are crawling with crackpot economists and you can't be too careful. So let me, by proxy, prove that I'm sane and we're on the right track here.

And anyway, given my bias, perhaps I should recuse myself from the argument I'm about to make. You see, on our first date, I impressed the woman who is now my wife by convincing her conservative brother-in-law that budget deficits are not always a problem. Such is DC romance.

So why don't I tell you about a wonderful talk I attended in 2007 by Joseph Stiglitz, Nobel laureate in economics and a guy with some very deep economic credentials?[16] What's unique about Stiglitz is not that he always rejects conventional wisdom—he doesn't. It's that he looks at it in the context of the real world and often finds it lacking.

In both his talk and his writings, he seems genuinely and appropriately worried about a mania for balancing budgets. If I could summarize his message in one overarching thought, it would be this: Too often, our budget debates mindlessly assume that deficit reduction is the best option, both for us and for other countries with whom we do business. This simplistic, reductionist view is leading both political parties toward a philosophy of fiscal austerity that will have very negative consequences.

The debate is far from academic. Misguided thinking about deficits has led to the two options that form the core of the fiscal debate between Democrats and Republicans: The Ds want to balance the budget by holding down spending and letting (some of) the Bush tax cuts expire; the Rs want to do so by extending the Bush tax cuts and cutting spending, big time. Make no mistake, when some candidate tells you how he wants to "save entitlements," he means he wants to save them by shrinking them. These two options have crowded out the third: raise the tax revenue we need to support that which will make our economy and country stronger.

Stiglitz framed the issue in terms of two pressing problems: a short-term one and a long-term one. The talk occurred at a time when the economy was growing about one point below its trend (with real GDP growth around 2 percent per year instead of 3 percent), a problem Stiglitz attributed mostly to the slump in housing and the loss of stimulus from that sector. In this context, taking money out of the economy by pursuing deficit reduction would do more harm than good.

You don't hit someone when they're down, and you don't pursue deficit reduction when the economy is already stressing out. As Stiglitz noted, "The idea that deficit reduction leads to a strong economy was an idea that Andrew Mellon tried in the midst of the Great Depression . . . the effect, of course, was not positive. Then came Keynesian economics."

In that current context, Joe was referring to what was hopefully a short-term problem and one that even some pretty hawkish folks on the deficit would be OK with. The more important question is the longer-term one: What's the proper role of deficit spending in good times?

Here's where reductionism—a zombie-like allegiance to balancing the budget—is your enemy. Stiglitz argued that "we should never focus just on deficits, but on broader economic concepts." What's the magnitude of the deficit relative to GDP (at the time, it was headed down to a very manageable 1 percent)? What are we spending it on (we were wasting far too much of it on the war and tax cuts for the rich instead of accumulating worthwhile assets)? Are we, in the interest of balancing the budget, ignoring important investments that the private sector won't make?

It's on this last point where I thought Stiglitz's message was most important, and it's where we're furthest off track. We have big and growing needs for investments that market forces simply won't make. We would be much wiser to focus on these deficits: segments of our population who need better access to education; early-childhood development and education; our public health care system, which will absolutely need to expand in coming years as the private, employer-based system unravels; safety nets, programs like unemployment insurance and job training that can help those displaced by globalization; and, one that Stiglitz emphasized, environmental policy.

More than any prominent economist, Stiglitz understands the damaging limits of fiscal austerity, and the extent to which it undercuts our ability to tackle the big problems of today and tomorrow, from frayed safety nets to depleted ozone, from the war on poverty to the war in Iraq.

Crunchpoint: Sure, I get it. When the Crunch guy says some deficit spending is fine, you hit me with a big "maybe." When the big-shot Nobelist says it, it's true. Oh well . . . no harm, no foul. I'm just glad to be on the same page with such a great thinker.

- **How liberating!**
  The federal budget,
  A place for our values.

How much of the U.S. economy is driven by the military-industrial complex?

Of course, this presumes the existence of the MIC (military-industrial complex), and, as we say in DC, "I can neither confirm nor deny . . ." Oh, hell, sure I can. Yes, there is an MIC, by which I mean there are powerful forces (see principle #1) that—in the name of national security—steer money their way, money that would be better spent elsewhere. More specifically, we're talking about private firms that sell to the U.S. military and the lobbyists that work for them—that's the MIC.

How much money? In 2006, we spent over $600 billion on national defense, representing about 5 percent of GDP and about a fifth of our national budget, more than Social Security or Medicare.[17] Now, 5 percent of GDP doesn't sound like much, and in fact, while that's up from 4 percent in 2000, it's down from 7 percent in the late 1980s, after the Reagan buildup, and 10 percent in the late 1960s, during Vietnam.

This is the constant refrain you will hear if you stumble into a DC hearing room, where Congress members get terribly tough with military budget requesters before they sign the blank checks. But in the words of the Congressional Progressive Caucus (CPC), a group of pols that really do want to spend less on war and weapons, just because we *can* spend the money doesn't mean we should.

There are three questions an economist evaluating this issue would ask:

1. Are the level and composition of these expenditures the best way to promote our security?

My research says no. I'm not an expert, but I know the work of a guy who is. Lawrence Korb, a former assistant secretary of defense under Reagan—how's that for street cred?—elaborates a series of cuts with reference to specific weapon systems that are being kept on life support by the pols and contractors feeding the MIC, not by any realistic rationale for our security.[18]

This is a guy who can tell you why we don't need a bunch more F/A-22 Raptors because they were built to offset the next generation of Soviet MIGs, which were themselves never built (by the way, I think these are all airplanes). Or why the DDG 1000 Zumwalt Class Destroyer (this one's a boat) is redundant; or how the C-130J transport aircraft have failed to meet contract specifications and cannot do what we bought them to do: transport troops and equipment into combat zones. Korb says we could save $60 billion a year by shifting resources away from these and other bad military investments.[19]

2. What are the "opportunity costs" of these expenditures?

Ah, that old chestnut, principle #3. What are these expenditures crowding out? The best way to answer that is to turn to the CPC's alternative budget, the one that takes the MIC dividend and allocates it in ways that would produce big, albeit nonexplosive, bangs for the bucks. They invest $30 billion a year for 10 years to develop renewable-energy resources, creating three million new jobs along the way. They fully fund the State Children's Health Insurance Program (SCHIP), to make sure that every eligible child gets publicly provided health insurance (the program is a proven success but it's getting crowded out by defense spending). They restore the cuts made to job training programs, K–12 education, community investments, food stamps, veteran's benefits, and housing.

The fact that these investments in our people go wanting so that we can build wasteful systems that even defense experts don't want is a national disgrace. But if you wanted to put such sentiments aside and just do steely-eyed economic analysis, you'd end up at the same place. The true economic cost of the MIC-induced waste is the productivity, health, education, and energy independence we lose from making the wrong spending choices.

3. What would happen if we cut back?

This gets to the heart of the question posed above: Would the economy stumble if we cut the cash infusions to the MIC? Very unlikely, given the answers to questions 1 and 2. Experts tell us that we would be better protected if we spent less on wasteful, outdated systems. And some of those dollars could be better spent on productivity-enhancing services, like better worker training and renewable-energy R&D. All told, the result of fighting the MIC would be likely to make us more secure and more productive.

So why is it so hard to turn swords to ploughshares; to leave the gun biz for the butter biz? Obviously, vested interests. But you don't get how deeply vested these interests are until you bump up against them. Even former Secretary of Defense Donnie Rumsfeld, a veritable tiger in his own right, to his credit tried to cut back on some of the waste at the Pentagon and didn't get anywhere. You have to recognize how deep these guys are into the public till. In late 2006, one MIC lobbyist told me that if the Iraq War were to end tomorrow, his firm would still be billing the U.S. government for 10 years to replace stuff we lost or left over there.

Leading me to this conclusion: If defense spending is to be kept from crowding out much else, it's going to come from grassroots, bottom-up pressure. I wrote a couple of articles about these issues in early 2007,[20] and got a tremendous response—requests to go on the radio all over the country, and, my personal favorite, a "go-get-'em" phone call from Ben Cohen, of Ben & Jerry's ice cream, who is a huge activist on this issue (he gives a demo on it using Oreo cookies, and afterward you get ice cream). A lot of people are plenty fired up about this, but what can be done? I speak to that fundamental question in the concluding chapter.

Crunchpoint: The MIC, a concept introduced in the 1950s, is alive and well. Don't let anyone tell you that it's no biggie since we spend only 5 percent of GDP on defense. It's not making us more secure, and it is crowding out better spending priorities.

Lots of people asked this related question: "How can we and why do we spend so freely on the war on terror?"

Like the many people who asked me to address this question, I've been struck and unsettled by how quickly and easily Congress writes a check whenever somebody invokes "the troops" or "the war on terror." Why is it that our representatives can easily raise endless amounts of money for war but can't adequately fund other stuff that people also care about, like schools, safety nets, social insurance, and public works? Yes, the MIC pushes them in that direction, but why don't other forces, ones represented by a lot more people, push back the other way?

You know how crime novels always say, "Follow the money"? Well, here's a very important variation on that (it's also a variation on principle #3 regarding trade-offs). Learn this well if you want to get what's going on in these seemingly arcane but vitally important spending debates: *Those who control the budget constraint, controls the debate.*

Whoever dictates what we can and can't afford controls the purse strings. When someone in power says, "We can afford X; we can't afford Y," prick up your ears and get ready to ask some tough questions. Much more often than not, the answer to "Why X, not Y?" is an elaborate version of "Because I say so."

In 2007, the *Washington Post* ran an important article documenting the loss of child care subsidies to low-income working parents.[21] One of the lessons from the welfare reform agenda of the 1990s was that such work supports are a critical component of a pro-work, anti-poverty agenda. But because the program is terribly underfunded—fewer than a fifth of eligible people receive help paying for child care—there's a huge waiting list, and families are left to give up on work or patch together less-than-desirable child care situations.

Let's look at the relative magnitudes of the costs in play here. Out of a $3 trillion federal budget, we spend about $5 billion a year at the federal level on child care. Because we don't add to these amounts for either inflation or population growth over time, the demand for child care slots is outpacing capacity. According to the Bush administration's own budget that year (2007), the failure to address this shortfall means that by 2010, the families of 300,000 children will not get the help they need.

I'm not at all suggesting that funding subsidized child care is the great, liberating strategy to get America back on track. I'm just using this one example as a microcosm of the way budget constraints and power play out in our world, with life-altering consequences.

Now, turn from butter to guns. The Congressional Budget Office—scorekeepers for such things—documented $600 billion as the cumulative price tag for Iraq, Afghanistan, and the "war on terror" from 2001 to 2007.[22] This will ramp up to well over $700 billion by 2008, as Congress signed off on the largest supplemental funding bill (a budget request over and above the annual budget) ever requested by a presidential administration: just shy of $100 billion, mostly for the war on terror and its sundry components. Congress did harrumph for a few weeks, but, as they did with every other supplemental request, they soon folded and signed the check.

Here's another dimension of the story. At the same time all of this negotiating was going on, I testified before the Senate Finance Committee on the question of whether there needed to be $8 billion worth of tax cuts to businesses to offset the impact of the federal minimum wage increase.[23] The idea that businesses, which had enjoyed about $300 billion in tax cuts over the past decade, needed $8 billion more to offset the first federal minimum wage increase in a decade was already nuts.

But in this context, that's not the point. Because of budget rules then in play, the senators had to raise $8 billion from other areas of the budget to pay for the tax cuts. During the course of the hearing, the senator in charge of the committee, Max Baucus (D-Montana), asked us what we thought of the deal. I made the glaringly obvious observation that if they could come up with $8 billion, I could think of a lot better stuff to use it for than needless tax cuts, prompting the senator to move on to the next witness with impressive speed.

No one should ever be fooled by "We can't afford it." When they want to, Congress can find the money. Of course, we can't have guns, butter, and whatever else with no regard for footing the bill. But the choices of how much revenue and expenditures we desire are exactly that: choices. In the world we need to strive for, they are priorities to be made by society through an open political process, where no one has the clout to preempt debate by saying, "This, not that."

The problem we now face, as put by Lawrence Mishel, an economist (and colleague) who really gets this stuff, is "the direct consequence of maintaining other priorities. Some [policymakers] are wedded to maintaining the recent tax cuts. Many more believe we have to spend whatever it takes for the wars in Iraq and Afghanistan. . . . Others believe that moving toward a balanced budget is essential. Whatever one thinks of these positions, it is clear that the result is that human capital investments get the leftover fiscal scraps."[24]

How does all of this inform the question about the opportunity costs of war? Sure, if you're spending around $11 billion a month on wars, it's harder to fund other priorities.[25] But as the tax-cut examples reveal, that's not what's blocking other options. The only thing standing between federal politicians and the types of public investments that will make this a better country is our own, self-imposed sense of disenfranchisement. I'm not for a moment suggesting that we all share the same priorities. I am instead confidently asserting that the majority of us share the desire to dramatically restructure government taxing and spending priorities in ways that favor productive investments in people and families and eschew bellicose adventurism.

Crunchpoint: The reason we spend so freely on war and so reticently in other areas is that the people controlling the money, regardless of party, are not expressing the priorities of the majority. This is surely because to most people, government spending seems either impenetrably boring or wholly divorced from their lives—or both. But once you spend a little time with the types of facts I just elaborated, a pervasive sense of terribly misguided priorities descends over your consciousness, and you recognize the tragedy in terms of wasted opportunities. And that is the first step back on the path to taking control of spending priorities.

- **The economist . . .**
  I listen as he tells me
  What I cannot have.

The Budgetary Crunchpoint in the News

At around the same time as the information cited above appeared, one of the *Washington Post*'s influential opinion writers, Robert Samuelson, a guy whose economic views are pretty typical (that is, conservative), wrote that "budget consequences should occupy a minor spot in our debates. It's not that the costs are unimportant; it's simply that they're overshadowed by other considerations that are so much more important. We can pay for whatever's necessary." [26]

As a friend of mine used to quip whenever I agreed with him: "That's what I'm sayin'!" It's not that we should ignore budget constraints, which are of course real and binding. But, once again, it's good old principle #3—economics is about trade-offs, and when someone says, "We can't afford training or child care subsidies," the right responses are: "Says who?" and "What are we spending the money on instead?"

Because, you see, *Samuelson was talking about the war in Iraq*. It's important to read his piece, because it's a great example of an economic analyst stating with deep authority what we can and can't afford, as if no value judgment was invoked.

And Samuelson's right. We can pay for whatever's necessary, including quality job training and child care. The problem is, his priorities, like those of many economic elites, are far out of step with those of the rest of us who foot the bills.

51

It seems like many Americans suffer from the lack of good jobs. Can we have a WPA (Works Progress Administration) again as we did under FDR?

Yes, we can and should create good, useful jobs in the public sector to boost the living standards of the least advantaged, but that's a much-smaller-scale endeavor than the WPA.

Public job creation under FDR took place during the Great Depression, the largest market failure in our modern history, when unemployment was around 25 percent. Today, it tends to hover around 4 to 6 percent. There's simply no need to intervene on that scale.

But while massive market failures are thankfully not part of our current economic landscape, intensive little market failures are much more common than we like to realize. They tend to affect particular groups in particular places, like young men with at most high school degrees in the rust belt, or minority youth. Even in 2000, when national unemployment was 4 percent, the share of young African-American male high school dropouts with a job was 38 percent. Other research has shown that over 70 percent of young men with these characteristics were jobless or incarcerated in the mid-2000s.[27]

Those, I'm afraid to say, are not recessionary numbers—they're deep depression numbers, and as I've stated, there is great precedent for such interventions in depressions. It's a relatively small group of particularly disadvantaged people, but these boats are unlikely to be lifted much by any tide. They need extra help.

Some would argue that they need school more than a job, but I'd say they need both. It's not just the WPA—we've had other moments in our history when the government created public sector jobs. In the 1970s, the Comprehensive Employment and Training Act helped to create some jobs, but it was awfully top-down. Washington, DC sprinkled money on some community centers and didn't do much follow-up. We now know there are better, more localized ways to go about this.[28]

Crunchpoint: Yes, we can and should create jobs for people, but unless the economy hits the skids, we should do so for just a small, very disadvantaged group of persons.

Well, then, shouldn't we lobby against technological change that leads to the job loss, like those robotic voices on the phone (that is, get real people back on the job)?

No, we shouldn't fight back against "labor-saving" technology, even though it sometimes seems like it's "labor-screwing." I say this while in full agreement about those annoying phone menus. And just for the record, while we usually find that tech changes boost efficiency, I'm awfully hard-pressed to view those automated phone menus in that light. One can waste a lot of time on them, and I have wondered if they kill as much efficiency as they create.

Economists would generally bristle at the notion of fighting against technology to preserve jobs. We take a secret oath at the altar of capital investment and technological change, granting that whatever "transition costs" occur, well, in this the best of all possible worlds, they must be lived with. We then very snarkily ask if you'd rather go back to the horse and buggy.

But let's not go back there. Instead, let's ask what would happen if you tried to hold back the tide of tech change. First, you'd have to regulate the hell out of employers and producers, basically telling them they couldn't use this robot or that ATM or some other new technology. I'm not sure that's even constitutional (I doubt even Alan Shore would take the case[29]).

Second, some of these changes tap big efficiency gains and make us a lot more productive than we would otherwise be, freeing people up to either enjoy more leisure or do more interesting work. And, while I know this can go either way, some labor-saving tech changes can help to preserve the environment. I used to have to drive to the library to renew books. Now I do it online (and let's not even talk about the late fines I'm saving).

The problem comes when there are not enough good jobs to make up for the ones that technology replaces. In the globalization discussion in the next chapter around jobs leaving the country (like technology, trade displaces jobs), I talk about this problem in terms of the personal costs invoked when a laid-off factory worker moves over to the service sector. These costs are indeed steep, but the way to offset them is not to block technological progress; instead, it is to tap the benefits of that progress to create better jobs for everyone.

It sounds utopian, but in fact it's prosaic. Once again, it comes down to ensuring that the benefits of faster productivity growth, itself very much a function of tech change, are broadly shared. If we, for example, put in place a system of universal health care and pensions (beyond Social Security, which, while an important leg of the retirement stool, cannot hold it up alone), we would immediately improve the quality of the majority of jobs in America that fail to provide these critical functions in a secure way that workers can count on.

Crunchpoint: We should resist the temptation to avoid labor-saving technology, and we should use the benefits from implementing it to improve job quality for all.

4

The World Ain't Flat
As All That

I'm glad the economy is more global now than ever before. I personally think it's exciting to contemplate the implications of connectedness—the fact that ideas, people, money, food, books, products, parts, energy, and gazillions of gigabytes of ones and zeros now transverse the globe with unimaginable speed. As a parent of two children adopted from China, I wake up every day in a global household, often much earlier than I'd like. And as an economist, I appreciate the opportunity that globalization affords the less advantaged to improve their living standards, their health, and their personal and societal potential through trade.

OK, that was all heartfelt and true, but I'm done channeling Thomas Friedman. Globalization is all of the above, but it's also part of the crunch we're deconstructing here. That is, to understand all sides of this issue, you've got to analyze globalization in the context of early-21st-century, American-style economics, where principle #1—power is a key economic determinant—dominates. The problem is that the minute you start to do so, some economic zealot wants to label you a protectionist and cast you from the temple.

That's not, of course, what we're about here in *Crunchland*. What follows is a balanced look at the issue of how globalization is playing out in our lives, from buying a ridiculously cheap music system, to jobs lost to trade, to a scintillating analysis of international exchange rates. Like it says in principle #2, things don't always play out the way economic theory says they will, and globalization is a many-faceted example of exactly that.

What's so right and/or wrong about globalization? Am I really hurting American workers if I buy cheap imports? Should I feel lousy about this? Am I supposed to oppose trade deals? Isn't our loss the gain of some poor person "over there" who probably needs the money even more than we do?

Settle in. Comfortable? This is going to take a few minutes.

First, allow me to share my latest encounter with the economics of globalization.

I'm a music lover and a critical listener, so when I finally got out of grad school, paid off some debts, and had a little real money, I bought, for many hundreds of dollars, a kickin' stereo. The components were very high quality and lasted for decades. I had to buy a CD player at some point—that medium didn't exist when I bought my system—but otherwise, I hadn't bought any electronic music equipment in about 25 years.

Well, I guess I blasted "Purple Haze" one too many times, and the speakers finally died of old age (the big, clunky tuner is as healthy as ever and is living in my attic—I should give it to the Smithsonian). So I headed out to the big box electronics store to get a new high-quality system.

Not having been in the market for such an item for so many years, I wasn't sure how much money I was going to need to spend, but I mentally put aside at least $500. That was already a few hundred less than I had spent on my old system in nominal dollars. In real dollars—adjusted for inflation since then—it was probably half as much.

Here's the clincher: Barring the purchase of a personal recording studio, I couldn't find a way to pay anywhere close to the amount I'd put aside. I found amazing systems, one of which now sits on my bookshelf, for the mid-hundreds of dollars. (The "I" in that last sentence is literal. The salesperson who helped me in this Best Buy store literally couldn't figure out how to turn the thing on. I'm not just being snotty—I come back to this point later in the book in a discussion of the big box retailer

The World Ain't Flat As All That

Circuit City). Oh, by the way, the next day I saw the same system advertised on sale for $20 less, and Best Buy made up the difference. I think I ended up paying about $130 for the system.

So, you don't have to look far to see the benefits of globalization. In economic terms, globalization—defined here as the increased flow across borders of goods, services, people, and ideas—by increasing the supply of stuff, lowers prices. There are other benefits, of course, accruing both to us and to our trading partners, but for all the lofty talk about expanded trade building bridges to the future and intertwining the fates of countries, most of us encounter and benefit from globalization in much the same way as I did that day.

And clearly, I don't think there's anything wrong with buying cheap imports. Yet, in these questions posed by a friend in San Francisco, my spiderlike senses pick up a murmur of guilt, mixed in with a lot of confusion.

That's not surprising. The U.S. trade debate generates a whole lot more heat than light.

Economists, policymakers, and the punditry are forever going on about the benefits of trade and the horrible folly of protectionism. In large part, they're motivated by two points, only the first of which is valid. That's the principle of *comparative advantage*, a great and centuries-old insight showing that trading partners both end up better off when they specialize in what they do best, even if their best isn't all that great.[1]

The other motivation, the one that generates all kinds of undesirable yet avoidable outcomes, is the belief that more trade always makes everyone better off.

Journalist Eric Alterman, in a piece in *The Nation* titled "Dude! Where's My Debate?" notes that the afore mentioned Thomas Friedman, a highly influential and breathless booster of "free trade" (the quotes are important, as you'll see), was asked if there was any free-trade agreement he'd oppose.[2] Friedman, a guy you would never think of as thoughtless, responded, "No, absolutely not," adding, "You know what, sir? I wrote a column supporting the CAFTA, the Caribbean Free Trade initiative. I didn't even know what was in it. I just knew two words: 'free trade.'"

It's worse. He didn't even get the name right: It's the Central America

Free Trade Agreement. This guy owns some of the most influential intellectual real estate in the world: He writes two op-ed essays a week for the *New York Times*. His books are everywhere. Yet because he's so thoroughly convinced that free trade is always a big winner and that legislation like CAFTA promotes it, he brags that he doesn't even have to look under the hood.

That's a shame and a disservice to the debate. And, thankfully, as the untruths of the free-trade uber alles boosters have become clearer to more people, there is now a debate on these issues.

To join that debate, it's helpful to consider the five myths of globalization:

1. You could stop it or even slow it down much.

The globalization horse is way far out of the barn, and trade agreements have much less to do with its pace than people like Friedman seem to think. Thirty-five years ago, trade volume amounted to 10 percent of our economy; now it's 30 percent (that's exports plus imports as a share of GDP). The fastest-growing exporter to the United States is China, and we don't have any trade treaty with them.[3] Like any other legal negotiation, these trade deals, like NAFTA (the North American Free Trade Agreement) and CAFTA, create a structure that generates winners and losers, with rules that protect some groups relative to others. NAFTA, for example, created lots of opportunities for investors but did little to ensure that workers in any of the three countries would reap the benefits of the agreement.

So trade deals have little to do with whether globalization goes forward. Regardless of these deals, countries will continue to expand trade relations. But that by no means suggests we should ignore trade deals. To the contrary, we need a new architecture, and by "we," I mean workers the world round (see myth #5).

2. Globalization is wonderfully benign; or it's all pain, no gain.

Like I said, for years the cheerleaders have derailed the debate, but you also need to be balanced here. You would be hard-pressed to find someone who has not saved some serious money thanks to expanded trade.

Nor can anyone deny that there are lots of smart people in other coun-tries who have great new opportunities thanks to globalization.

But you don't have to look too far to see the pain either. Since 2000 alone, we've lost over three million jobs in manufacturing, in no small part due to our unbalanced trade—we import a ton more than we sell abroad. And now, with the offshoring (more on offshoring below) of white-collar jobs, the downward pressure on wage growth is hitting sec-tors that were previously inoculated. You know all those satellites and fiber-optic cables carrying ones and zeros all over the globe? Well, if your work can be represented by those ones and zeroes, it can be crammed into those nifty cables, and guess what? Don't matter whether you're a scholar or a fool, you're now in competition with smart, cheap people in faraway places.

And all that stuff about low prices? It's true, but remember, the story of stagnant American wages and incomes for so many workers in the mid-dle and lower rungs of the scale is an inflation-adjusted story—that is, these wages are adjusted for the price-inducing benefits of trade, and they're still falling. In the horserace of low prices versus low wages, wages still sometimes lose.

3. Its costs and benefits are broadly shared.

Would it were so. In fact, estimates are that U.S. trade with low-wage countries explains 20 to 30 percent of the increase in wage inequality over the past generation.[4] That's less than half, so you could say it's not a smoking gun, but there are no single factors that explain more. Global-ization, American style, is one reason why our economy has become more unequal.

4. Its downsides only affect displaced workers.

It is now de rigueur to acknowledge that—who knew?—a small group of losers are genuine victims of globalization. It's just a few hard-hatted dinosaurs from the rust belt, but hey, I'm sensitive . . . I recognize that an egg or two had to get broken to make this global omelet.

Wrong. While folks whose jobs actually and visibly went overseas may be the most recognizable victims, tens of millions of incumbent workers—men and women still at work—have lower wages today than they would if trade were more balanced. My colleague Josh Bivens, an economist, estimates that increased trade has cost the typical household about $2,000 over the past generation. That's not a huge dent, but it's not trivial either (and remember, this is a net calculation—it accounts for the low-price effect).[5]

5. Its outcomes cannot be shaped. They must be accepted as is.

Once you get that trade deals have little effect on globalization (barring, of course, crazy ideas that wouldn't fly, like huge tariffs), you are free at last to get smart, creative, and compassionate. Maybe most important, given that their regimes want access to our markets, here's where we might be able to help the downtrodden in poor countries.

Instead, as Bivens puts it, "Today, access to the U.S. market is contingent upon the developing world adopting a host of policies that map awfully conveniently to what the international corporate class wants."[6]

Why, exactly, is labor so cheap in what the trade literature calls "less developed countries"? The economist would answer that it's because their workers are plentiful, with low value added; and, though Chinese productivity, for example, is growing faster than ours, there's something to that.[7] But lest we get too cozy with our cheap stuff, let us not forget that political repression is another reason. As long as they want access to our markets—and believe me, they do—we should use that leverage to insist on the granting of workers' rights.

It would thus be a real advance if these trade deals devoted less ink to protecting "intellectual property rights" of first-world producers and more to the rights of workers in developing countries. One good reason to get behind globalization is that we'd like to see the world's poor realize some of the prosperity that expanded trade is supposed to generate. When we play overly nicely with repressive governments—when we essentially make exclusive deals between their big investors and our big investors—we sacrifice this opportunity.[8] Does all this mean we should smugly blast Jimi Hendrix on our cheap but awesome sound systems, slipping into a purple haze while we forget about globalization's downsides?

Of course not. As I discuss in Chapter 5, there's lots we could do here to offset the downsides without sacrificing the upsides.

Crunchpoint: I know it took a while to get here, but the answer is, there's lots that's right and wrong about globalization. Cheap imports help us as consumers but hurt us as workers. Trade deals are not just about globalization, they're also about power, and they should stop protecting investors at the expense of workers, here and abroad.

■ **Globalization!**
Such low, low prices, and yet . . .
my pay lags behind.

Is there anything good about having jobs go out of the country?

First, let me say that this is a great question. For one, it doesn't assume that something that sounds bad—jobs leaving the country—is bad. (Principle #2: Things are not always as they seem in this biz.) Second, it provides us with a good opportunity to explore an important shortcoming of conventional economic analysis.

Third, the original question included a verse from the Bruce Springsteen song "My Hometown":

Now Main Street's whitewashed windows and vacant stores
Seems like there ain't nobody wants to come down here no more
They're closing down the textile mill across the railroad tracks
Foreman says these jobs are going boys and they ain't coming back to your hometown

That may be so, but the conventional economic wisdom is that it's no big deal if jobs leave the country, because of two assumptions and a caveat: (a) we always benefit from expanded trade with other countries, (b) we're always at full employment, meaning that there are always enough jobs to go around, so no biggie if some go elsewhere, and (c) even if it were bad, trying to stop it would be worse.

So, economic wisdom contradicts the Boss—who you gonna believe?

They're both right, up to a point, but the Boss is more right. We've lost lots of jobs—and some very good jobs—probably forever. They ain't comin' back to your or my hometown. On the other hand, the unemployment in 2006 was 4.6 percent, pretty darn low, so something else is going on, too. (By the way, Harry Truman allegedly asked for a one-handed economist, to avoid having to hear statements like that.)

Behind the lyrics is our growing trade deficit, but "negative net exports of 6 percent of GDP" is hard to work into a song. We buy a whole lot more manufactured goods from abroad, from cars to steel to baseballs, than we export, and there are real jobs embodied in that trade deficit. As noted earlier, over the course of the business cycle that began in March 2001, we've lost about three million factory jobs.

At the same time, we've gained about seven million jobs in the service sector. So we're net gainers on the jobs front. But to get to the core of your question, we have to ask about the relative quality of the jobs both lost and gained.

Factory workers who go over to the services usually lose a lot. We're often talking here about moving someone from a high-productivity, unionized job with high-tier wages and fringes to a sector that's less productive, has much less collective bargaining, and has a much wider dispersion of compensation. Recent research into the consequences of layoffs reveals that just under three-quarters of reemployed factory workers suffer a real pay cut, and for 40 percent, it's a cut of at least 20 percent.[9]

What do we gain from trade? In the context of jobs, trade helps to lower prices and expand economic activity in other areas. You need people to distribute and sell all those cheaper goods, and that's partly behind the jobs numbers above as well as the lousy wage results—Wal-Mart simply wouldn't exist as we know it in the absence of all this global trade, but they're not exactly creating Cadillac jobs.

You also need people here to do higher-end work associated with this global model. Trade may send the factory over there, but we've often kept the white-collar work here. There are lots of financial analysts and high-level programmers whose work is complementary to these trade arrangements. Those are good jobs, but they're not the ones that Bruce, or anyone else, is singing about. Nor are they the ones going to the people he's singing about.

But there's new and telling development regarding the white-collar sector and trade: Thanks to the Internet, we've started trading more in white-collar services. It's called *offshoring*, and it comes down to this: If your work can be digitized or routinized, no matter how well educated you are, there may well be an equally smart person happy to look at that X-ray or write that computer code for about a tenth of what you make.

Now, don't get me wrong—the radiology practice isn't going the same way as the textile firm. But while offshoring hasn't had as much of an impact on jobs as trade in manufactured goods, it already appears to be playing a role in weakening higher-end wage growth (real college wages were up only 2 percent from 2000 to 2006). You can bet that this is getting a lot of people's attention. The traditional rap of the economic elites is that higher skills will insulate you from the job pressures of trade: "They'll take all those dirty, greasy factory jobs while the rest of us don white lab coats and point and click our way into a prosperous future." Who knew the Indians and Chinese could wear lab coats, too?

Where does this leave us? Given my avid nonprotectionist stance stressed in the last question, my view here might surprise you: We could and we should do a lot more to keep jobs from leaving the country. Not through trying to block global trade—as I stress in that discussion, you couldn't stop it if you wanted to—but through other ways, including leveraging other countries' desire to access our markets by insisting that our trading partners play fair, ending tax incentives to offshore, and investing in our manufacturing sector to get to work on any green alternatives we can think of.

Memo to Detroit: Europeans get 43 miles per gallon, we get 25. Fix it. Memo to the Chinese Gov't.: You want access? Stop blocking our exports and boosting your imports by depressing your currency relative to ours.

Crunchpoint: There's nothing good, per se, about losing jobs to other countries, but it's one of the outcomes of trade and globalization, and there are many upsides to these forces as well. The problem is that too often we're losing good jobs and getting lousier ones. We should push back aggressively against that, not by going into protectionism but by investing in improving the quality of service jobs, green manufacturing, and leveraging our market access to force others to play fair.

I do not understand the protectionism that runs rampant on the left. Aren't the Democrats the party that defends the oppressed? When it comes to buying stuff made in countries that are much poorer than ours, wouldn't basic morality dictate that the people in the third world need the business more than us?

What do you do with your free time? Me, I troll the blogosphere looking for really tough, contentious questions (I found this one on policy journalist Ezra Klein's blog).

Actually, the economics of a question like this are straightforward, commonsensical, yet largely unhelpful, which makes this a great example of how standard-issue economic analysis can let you down, and in doing so exacerbate the problem.

Such analysis makes no reference to morality or need. It tells you that if this generic good is made more cheaply abroad, which will typically be the case with manufactured goods, like toys, textiles, and electronics, then not only is our welfare enhanced if we buy it, but so is that of the exporter. Game over: Both sides win.[10]

Yet, the questioner suggests that protectionism "runs rampant on the left." I'm not sure that's true, but I will tell you this: There are a lot of very pissed off people who feel screwed by globalization. Many probably are, or were, more likely to support Democrats, so this may be where the questioner's perception is coming from.

In fact, these dynamics regarding globalization started showing up quite clearly in American politics in the mid-2000s. A couple of high-profile candidates, most notably Sherrod Brown from Ohio, now a Democratic senator, ran campaigns that were in large part targeted at those who felt betrayed by globalization. Despite near-unanimous support among political elites for "free trade," Brown consistently argued that if elected, he would vote against free-trade agreements.

That sounds protectionist, but what Brown and others, like Senator

Jim Webb (D-Virginia), another populist successful in 2006, are saying is that there are people here who need protection from globalization. Those people are voting for that message, and there are apparently enough of them to make a difference in our national politics.

How did that happen? Do the economists have this wrong?

In a word, yes, and that fact complicates the morality called for above. Allow me to be self-referential, and I suggest that you too try this at home. I happen to share this questioner's view: We're rich and they're poor, and the world would be well served if we became a little less rich and they became less poor. As noted earlier, one problem is that current trade arrangements don't accomplish this desirable goal, but that's beside the point here. Instead, we want to examine where the protectionism is coming from.

As I said, many of us would like to see globalization lift the living standards of the world's poor. But I am an economic elite in a position largely insulated from global competition (famous last words?). What if I were a former manufacturing worker who lost a union job with upper-middle-income wages and Cadillac benefits—a job that placed my family solidly in the middle class and financed the full set of middle-class aspirations? What if my new job paid 15 to 20 percent less on average (see last answer) and was a lot less likely to provide health or pension benefits? What if I had taken the advice of the punditry and got a college education, only to find myself in a white-collar occupation exposed to off-shoring competition (like programming or accounting)? How quickly would I—would you—recognize the morality of helping to lift the living standards of the poor over there versus the displaced here?

Those of us who bemoan "protectionism" need to recognize that for the first time in years, poll results reveal a majority of people worried that the next generation won't do as well as they did. One representative poll from March 2007 found that 69 percent of respondents said the "American Dream" will be harder to reach for the next generation.[11] Reporting on exit polls from the 2006 midterm elections, the New York Times wrote: "In exit polls on Election Day, fewer than one in three people said they expected life for the next generation of Americans to be better than life today."[12] A Pew Research Center poll from 2006 found that half of the respondents worried that children growing up today will be worse off than people are now.[13]

No matter how moral or caring we are regarding the plight of others, even those who suffer under terrible living standards, it is our nature to fiercely defend our children's economic prospects. When people come to believe that globalization, as it is currently playing out, is robbing them and, even more so, their children of their legitimate opportunities, they will do everything they can to *protect* themselves from such trends. We can call that *protectionism*, but it's not a dirty word in this context, and it won't stop anyone from pursuing ways to limit the damage.

By the way, people have a pretty nuanced view on these matters. In a poll from February 2007, about two-thirds agreed that trade was "good for the economy." But about half felt we've lost more from globalization than we've gained.[14] Sounds a little schizoid, yet it reflects the reality that expanded trade has surely led to faster overall economic growth than would otherwise be the case, but a lot of people feel it's not reaching them (what are the economic benefits of trade, anyway?—that's next).

Are they right? We've established that the economists have gotten this wrong, but does that mean the people are right?

With huge apologies for the squirrelly answer, yes and no. Consumers, voting with their wallets, have voted strongly in favor of expanded trade, just like I did when I bought my super-cheap music system. To get the slightest bit techie about it, at the micro-level we benefit from the increased supply of goods, which lowers prices. But the increased supply of workers producing the goods, and now services as well, puts downward pressure on wages. Those whose jobs and incomes have been or will be negatively affected by globalization, and we're talking about a majority of workers, recognize the price/wage horse race, and that justifiably makes them anxious.

Crunchpoint: The left isn't protectionist, at least not in the classical sense of isolation with no regard for suffering elsewhere. What you're seeing among Democratic policy makers is a rising recognition that many Americans need some form of protection from the downsides of globalization. This does not imply less trade, which would threaten gains to the poor elsewhere. To the contrary, these policy makers would like to craft trade deals that benefit poor workers in developing countries more than rich investors. But they also see the need for better safety nets and social insurance to protect our own workers. Without such protection, neither these politicians nor the workers they represent should be expected to cheerfully support a more expansive approach to trade.

Just how much do we gain from expanded trade with the rest of the world? [15]

We import a lot more than we used to—30 years ago, imports were about 10 percent of GDP; now they're 17 percent—and most of those goods are considerably cheaper than they would be if we made them here. I've seen credible estimates that this effect of trade can save a low-income family shopping at Wal-Mart over a thousand dollars in a given year relative to what it would have had to spend in a world that was under more restrictive trade policies.

Of course, there are costs as well, as discussed above, and in the case of Wal-Mart this same poor family can find itself facing tough job and wage pressures. But here, let us look exclusively at the gains from trade, because they've been highly distorted.

These days, even pure free traders have started to acknowledge trade's downsides. It might be that offshoring of skilled jobs got their attention—as long as it was those messy jobs in heavy industry whacking blue-collar guys, it was no biggie to the elites. But what seems to be going on here is that an ever-shrinking group can't let go of the fantasy that we all always benefit from expanded trade.

These guys are dangerous to their own cause and to the cause of properly managed globalization. Two guaranteed ways to make people unwilling to embrace further opening of the U.S. market to foreign trade on *any* terms are (1) deny that anybody is harmed by it and (2) make wildly distorted claims about its benefits.

In this way, the most enthusiastic cheerleaders for globalization as currently practiced are doing more than Lou Dobbs ever could to make the American public suspicious about seeing any benefits from trade. After all, genuinely good policies don't need a lot of exaggerations on their behalf.

Cheerleaders Sebastian Mallaby of the *Washington Post* and Fred Bergsten of the Peterson Institute for International Economics (IIE) are big-time offenders in this regard, and both tout a ridiculously large number regarding the prospective benefits of signing ever more trade agreements: $500 billion per year.

That number isn't off by just a little. It's about $480 billion above the high end of most conventional estimates. To get there, you have to cook the books—broil them, really—in a terribly unsavory manner. At the heart of the number is the assumption that the U.S. market, despite a relatively tiny number of actual tariffs, quotas, or other explicit legal restraints, is in reality hugely protectionist, blocking imports and foreign investment with insurmountable yet invisible barriers. The method assumes particularly high trade barriers in our service sector.

There are real gains from trade liberalization. Reasonable estimates range from $4 to $20 billion.

That's not nothing, and there are also gains to our trading partners from greater access to the U.S. market. However, globalization's current rules (the ones inspiring all the pom-pom waving) make this access inordinately costly to the world's developing nations. Essentially, the current rules grant access contingent upon these nations' adopting a range of economic policies that meet the desires of investors on both sides of the deal—like U.S.-style patent protections—while leaving the rights of workers out of the contract. The cheerleaders' advocacy campaign to ramp up this model of globalization isn't doing the world's poorest any favors.

And then there's the problem that no one in their right mind believes these hyperbolic claims. Even if they did, it would only leave them more convinced than ever that these benefits were eluding them and accumulating exclusively at the top of the income scale.

As noted above, polling data suggest that Americans have a fairly nuanced view of trade, one that I think reflects the reality. They get that trade is good for America but question how good it is for them.

Such results reflect the fact that increased trade, *just as economic theory predicts*, boosts growth but also has generated greater inequality. It's the obvious outcome of expanding trade with countries whose wages are a lot lower than our own. Further, as technology and the huge expansion of the global labor pool make a much wider range of jobs contestable by workers much poorer than those in the United States, trade's negative influence on wage growth here could balloon in the near future.

There are good, ambitious policy ideas for pushing back against these trends (see Chapter 5), including stronger social insurance and safety-net programs that reach higher up the wage scale, comprehensive reform of the rules governing globalization, and undertaking of the public investments needed to introduce more efficient and environmentally benign production in the U.S. economy.

But we'll never be able to craft a rational response that matches the scale of the dislocations of globalization if irrationalities and downside denials are rampant. After all, who needs to "solve" the problem of $500 billion magically created with merely "transitional" and trivial downsides?

Crunchpoint: Because estimates of the gains from trade end up falling prey to ideologues more interested in booster-ism than sound analysis, they range from single-digit billions to many hundreds of billions. The low end is the right one, and gains in the $10 billion range are indeed worthy. As for the ridiculously high-end estimates, could somebody please take the pom-poms away from these cheerleaders gone wild?

OK, I get that globalization generates both big costs and big benefits. But sometimes it seems like it's invoked to justify greed. Do you see that?

I do, and let me describe what I recently saw.

In spring 2007, the *Washington Post* ran a story about the electronics retailer Circuit City that nicely brought together many of these globalization themes and revealed the power dynamics that play such a determining role in who benefits from expanded trade.[16]

The retailer released a press statement full of the usual claims about how big changes would position the firm to make "improved and sustainable returns in today's marketplace," in which they also announced that they planned to lay off 3,400 sales associates. Such layoffs, though unfortunate, are a perfectly normal element of our turbulent markets, especially around restructurings. What's weird is that they said they were going to hire a new sales force at lower wages.

Talk about in-your-face management. I can absolutely see why a firm whose stock was down by a third over the past year would decide to make some big changes. But unless your workforce is truly overpaid, replacing a big chunk of it with lower-paid workers is a recipe for lousier service, fewer sales, and lower profits. At the time, many predicted that after the initial bump, stock prices would sink further. We were wrong, though. They never got that initial bump, and the stock just kept sliding, down 15 percent a few months later (while the overall stock market was up strong).

Scrimp on your sales staff—Circuit City graciously said the laid-off workers could apply for their old jobs at reduced pay after 10 weeks—and you're cutting off your nose to spite your face.

Circuit City said their staff was overpaid, but other reports confirm that the staff made close to the market average of around $11 an hour. That's barely a living wage. Circuit City thought they were being lean and mean, but they were just being mean, and it hurt them.

Remember principle #1, about power in economics? Well, power corrupts, and this is economic corruption. It's not illegal, but it is immoral. Traditional economists believe that the invisible hand guides our free market system to the most efficient outcomes, which often happen to be the most just outcomes as well. But when companies act in this manner, that pristine result stays on the textbook page. What we get in the real world is a group of clueless execs who I'm sure believe they were acting in their shareholders' best interest yet ended up hurting all parties involved.

Again, it's a small case, but it's a microcosm of a way of doing business that threatens to undermine much that's good and productive in our economy.

Instead of our usual *crunchpoint*, these events inspired the following view from the future—a memo from the Labor Department in the year 2057.

HOW THE CAPITALISTS KILLED CAPITALISM

Date: April 10, 2057

Memo: From the communitarian of labor

Topic: Historical musings regarding the dark ages

The seed of the destruction of the market economy that predominated until the early 21st century was planted in a 50-year-old press release from the electronics retailer Circuit City.

As was common in this dark period of our economic history, the firm announced a restructuring, claiming that the proposed changes would position them to make "improved and sustainable returns in today's marketplace." Part of the plan was to lay off 3,400 sales workers—again, not unusual as restructurings often involved "layoffs" (younger persons will not recognize the word—it was a practice wherein people were told they no longer had a job).

What was so unusual about this announcement, however, was Circuit City's claim that they were going to replace the laid-off workers with lower-wage workers (yes, back then employers simply decided what they would pay their workers).

Given the times, their rationale for undertaking big changes made sense. Their "stock price" (don't ask—it was a complicated form of legalized gambling) was down by a third. But despite their claims to the contrary, their workers already made the pretty low wage, and it was clear at the time that their tactic would backfire. As we predicted, their stock prices sank further, and they were soon out of business.

What's amazing here, and so revealing about the ultimate demise of the market economy, is that the firm thought it was a good idea to advertise this practice. They were a retailer with stores in people's neighborhoods, not some behind-the-scenes player. Did they really think this was the message consumers wanted to hear? Did they really believe people would shop at a place where their fellow citizens were treated this way?

From our secure vantage point of today, we view this as a good example of the economic corruption of the earlier regime. What Circuit City did was not illegal. To the contrary, traditional economists at the time believed that such actions led to the most efficient outcomes.

Lucky for us, they had it all wrong.

It helps us to see clearly how the capitalists killed capitalism. Somehow they failed to recognize that the concentration of income—in 2005 the top 1 percent of households controlled 22 percent of all income, the highest since 1929—was politically unsustainable. The unabashed free-trade advocates, by denying any downsides to globalization, sowed the seeds of protectionist measures that divided nations and killed the benefits of trade. The rabid opponents of social insurance, safety nets, minimum wages, and unions made it impossible for workers to claim their fair share of growth and gave rise to a level of economic insecurity amid growth that sealed those opponents' own dismal fate.

Now, through our MRS (massive redistribution system), the top 1 percent controls 1 percent of national income. We all have jobs for life, and our supreme leadership labor council decides what everybody gets paid. Perhaps we should thank our greedy forebears.

Coffee break's over. Everybody back to work . . . NOW!

Is it wrong to hire an undocumented worker to clean my house even if I pay her a decent wage? Am I hurting the job prospects of someone born here?

Yeah, I'd say it pretty much is wrong. Though, given your generous wage policy, you're not necessarily hurting native-born workers.

First of all, think about how this is going to play in your confirmation hearing for attorney general or something.

The real problem here is that nobody wins from winking at illegality. You might argue that the undocumented workers win, or they wouldn't take the job, but it's not that simple. And sure, it's good to pay people fairly, because it's the right thing to do (see Bible) and because higher-paid people tend to do better jobs. (As a dad who occasionally hires babysitters, I've never seen the sense in paying the minimum wage to people who look after our kids. We pay the 40th percentile wage, leaving sitters wondering why they're getting $12.56 an hour.)[17]

But while there are many tough issues in our immigration debate, this isn't one of them. Undocumented workers need to get on a path to citizenship, both for themselves and for the folks with whom they compete, be they native-born workers or other immigrants. By providing them with employment, you become part of the problem that badly needs a solution. Granted, you're not as big a part of the problem as a contractor with a staff of illegals, but that's just a matter of scale. (Of course, the challenge here is, how do you know if someone is undocumented? You could ask, but most of us aren't going to go there, and we couldn't tell forged papers from real ones if we did. The solution to this problem is discussed next.)

Undocumented workers in America live and work in a nowhere zone—an untenable and dangerous space where large swaths of people are angry and suspicious of them, and where employers exploit their labor without fear of retribution. The solution is to bring them out of the shadows and under the umbrella of the same labor protections, from minimum wage to overtime pay, that generally prevent legal workers from getting soaked. This helps them, of course, but by taking illegally low wages and lousy working conditions off the table, it also helps the folks with whom new immigrants compete. It's called "blocking the low road."

Crunchpoint: Accommodating illegality, even if everyone else does it, is ultimately a recipe for dysfunction. Undocumented workers need to become citizens, for their own good and for that of the folks they compete against. You shouldn't knowingly hire them.

I don't know what to make of the immigration debate. My instinct is to be welcoming to anyone seeking a better life, but the system, such as it is, really does seem broken. What's the best way to resolve this?

In my day job as a DC policy wonk, this issue of immigration is without a doubt the one that generates the most intense debate. The passions it stirs up are deep and can get ugly. They may be a vocal minority, but my read is that many Americans are pissed off about some aspect of the way immigration is playing out.

In fact, polling data reveal that a solid majority thinks we should be doing more to secure the borders. Still, the most visceral anger I've seen is among those who believe that immigrants are taking their jobs and wages.[18] You can argue, as I do, that the economic research tends to find surprisingly small effects—one authoritative study found that over the past 20 years, immigrant competition lowered the wages of the least educated native-born workers by about 5 percent over 10 years, which ain't nothing, but it ain't much, either.[19] Make this argument to someone who believes he or she has been hurt by such competition, though, and you come off like you're saying, "Who you gonna believe, me or your own eyes?"

Part of it is racism and nativism, but I think that's the least of it. Here's what I believe is the bigger motivating story: The tenor of this debate changes for the worse when the economic pickings are slim.

Have you ever wondered why we didn't have much of an immigration debate in this country in the 1990s? It wasn't because fewer immigrants were entering the workforce: Foreign-born workers increased their share faster in the 1990s than in earlier decades. It was because the rising economic tide was lifting all boats, whether they were rafts from Cuba or rowboats from Bayonne.

In the 2000s, we've had lots of economic growth, but it has flowed largely to those at the top of the scale, leaving natives and immigrants to fight it out over the crumbs. Also, over the last few decades, whole industries in parts of the country have become dominated by immigrants, including meatpacking and construction. Both of those industries used to be largely unionized sectors providing good-quality jobs. That's no longer the case.

No one should blame immigrants for these changes. But neither should we deny the experience of those who have watched it happen.

The question is, what's the best way forward?

The answer is to craft a realistic policy that satisfies these two broad criteria: We remain a welcoming nation, born of immigrants; and we regain control of our borders. The problem at this point is not immigration; it's the dysfunctional system of illegal immigration.

As Ray Marshall, former labor secretary and a wise man when it comes to this issue, puts it, immigration is an integral part of what makes this a great country. "*Unauthorized* immigration, on the other hand, subjects migrants to grave dangers and exploitation, suppresses domestic workers' wages and working conditions, makes it difficult to adjust immigration to labor market needs, perpetuates marginal low-wage industries addicted to a steady flow of unauthorized immigrants, is unfair to people waiting to enter the United States legally, and undermines the rule of law. The issue is not immigrants, but their legal status, characteristics, and integration into American life."[20]

So, we've got to try a lot harder to put a lid on undocumented flows into the country. And the only way to do that is to forget about walls and get serious about a system that authorizes workers. I hate to go to the Big Brother place, but we need to get between employers addicted to an endless flow of cheap labor and unauthorized immigrants for whom a substandard job here is a step up. We have the technology to implement a reliable system that tells employers whether they're hiring an illegal worker. What we have lacked thus far is the political guts to mete out serious punishment to those employers who ignore the law. Without that, true immigration reform will never occur.

Once we establish a worker authorization system with real penalties for violators, we grant some type of earned citizenship to those here already. Then we let citizenship do its thing—simply bestowing citizenship to those willing to play by our rules has been a great integrator for generations of immigrants.

One final piece of the puzzle that gets too little attention: The desire to leave your country is driven by both a pull and a push. We focus a lot on the pull—the demand for cheap labor here—but not enough on the push—the failure of poorer countries to provide decent opportunities to their own. We need to be careful not to create conditions in other countries that push the push—that is, conditions that diminish the opportunities for citizens to do well there, thus creating an incentive to come here. For example, NAFTA made it tougher for small Mexican farmers to compete, and many were forced to migrate north.[21] They may have been headed for the factories in northern Mexico, but once that didn't work out, many kept going.

Crunchpoint: Those who forget history are doomed to repeat overused maxims. Every immigration reform has foundered on one point: our failure to control immigrant flows and thus to prevent illegal immigration. We've failed because we've not had the political will to crack down on employers addicted to an endless flow of cheap labor. If we correct this—and it is well within our technological power to do so—we can legitimize a welcoming approach to immigration.

- **The immigrant . . .**
The American . . .
I wish them both success.

I **read lots of accounts of how we need more immigrants to relieve a shortage of workers. But do such shortages really exist? Can't we find enough people here already who need to work?**

As the immigration debate got hot in 2006–07, lots of articles starting showing up asserting that the immigrant flows were critically important to the U.S. job market, due to our pervasive labor shortages. In one typical article from spring 2007, for example, various captains of industry and their government reps complained about a shortage of willing applicants, skilled and "unskilled," to meet their needs.[22] "We do not have enough workers to support a growing economy," complained the U.S. Chamber of Commerce. The secretary of commerce claimed that without greater immigrant flows, "we will have significant labor shortages in key occupations." In their minds, more immigration is needed to offset an alleged labor shortage.

Sounds reasonable, but remember your principles: #3—there are trade-offs involved here, and to ignore them is to ignore the economic needs of folks already here, immigrant and native-born worker alike; #1—there's a power play here, too. That is, there are distributional outcomes that benefit some and hurt others.

As I've stated throughout, there are all kinds of great reasons to support welcoming policies toward legal immigrants. Based on what they can earn here compared with what they can earn at home, they're much better off, and immigrants have obviously played an integral role in our economy and society since day one. But while offsetting labor shortages may sound like a good idea, it's usually not.

Consider this when you hear the "labor shortage" complaint: If there's really a shortage, the price of the thing in short supply should rise. In this case, we're talking about the wage of the worker in the shortage occupation. In fact, such wage movements represent an important mechanism in free-market economies like ours. It's called a *price signal*, and it signals workers in other occupations, ones that might be contracting, to shift over to the ones where they're needed. If you jam this signal by artificially inflating supply, you damage the structure of economic returns in the job market, which leads to greater levels of income inequality. Sound familiar?

One thing we learned in the 1990s was that a surefire way to reconnect the fortunes of working people at all skill levels, immigrant and native-born alike, to the growing economy is to let the job market tighten up. A tight job market pressures employers to boost wage offers to get and keep the workers they need. One equally surefire way to short-circuit this useful dynamic is to turn on the immigrant spigot every time some group's wages go up (note the fanciful assumption that we can control immigrant flows—as I stressed above, however, that's both doable and essential to successful reform. To do so—to solve every labor shortage by bringing in more workers from abroad—may boost profits, but it also jams an important economic signal, squeezes paychecks, and contributes to the crunch.

Finally, economist Dean Baker makes a relevant point here: why do we protect high-wage occupations from immigrant competition?[23] Doctors, accountants, lawyers, and even economists (while patting ourselves on the back for eschewing protectionism) use professional, educational, and licensing requirements to keep the flow of competitors from abroad to a trickle. This helps keep their labor a scarce commodity, raises their wages, and raises the prices of their services to the rest of us. Apparently, we understand the value of tight labor markets for these high-end workers. We ought to do so for others as well.

Crunchpoint: When you hear someone say, "We can't find the workers we need," make sure he or she's not leaving off the rest of the sentence: "at the wage we're willing to pay." And if labor's in short supply, then let it be. There's nothing wrong with a labor shortage that a good, old-fashioned wage boost can't cure.

What's all this about the "strength of the dollar"? Does this have any impact on my day-to-day life? Don't we want a strong dollar? Sure sounds better than a weak one.

You're reasonably thinking: strength, good; weakness, bad. But remember basic principle #2: Economic relationships aren't always what they seem. In this case, as in pretty much every other case, how the strength of the dollar affects you depends on who you are.

First, what is a strong dollar? Is it one that's hard to tear asunder? No, it's one whose value is high relative to that of currencies from other countries. Dollar strength has meaning only in this international context. If one dollar used to get you one British pound and now it gets you two, then the dollar has gotten stronger relative to the British pound.

Second, yes, it does affect your day-to-day life, because a strong dollar means cheaper imports. One reason why big box retailers like Wal-Mart are able to sell you a lifetime supply of socks for a few bucks is that the strong dollar goes a long way with their overseas suppliers.

So, what's wrong with that?

Well, cheap imports mean expensive exports. A strong dollar makes it tougher for us to sell our products abroad, and it's one of the reasons why we've got trade deficits (exports minus imports) up the wazoo. It's also a reason why we've lost over three million jobs in manufacturing since 2000.

You may be thinking there are a lot more consumers than manufacturers, so shouldn't we opt for a strong dollar? Not so fast, for a couple of reasons.

First, while it's tempting to envision America as a bunch of computer programmers and nano-technologists wearing spotless lab coats, as opposed to greasy overalls, pointing and clicking their way into the future, a strong manufacturing base is really important to this country. It's a highly productive sector, one responsible for major innovations in auto, airplane, steel, textile production, and even computer technology. In large part because of the productivity differential, our factories provide good jobs, with high value added contributing to above-average wages and benefits.

Here's the real kicker: If we want to buy more stuff from abroad, we've got to sell more stuff abroad. That is, you finance your trade deficit by raising exports, lowering imports, or some combination therein. Sure, we can grow more slowly and suck in fewer imports, and that might be OK, but it just amplifies our need for more manufacturing capacity to shift production back here.

Second, you're probably, and reasonably, thinking that you spend a lot of your money on imports, so if they go up in price, you're screwed. In fact, as some colleagues and I show in a research paper, cheap imports like the ones you buy at Wal-Mart make up a much smaller share of your budget than they used to, and it's not just because they're cheaper. It's because health care, housing, college, child care—stuff we'll never import—is more important, and more expensive.[24] On average, we spend 17 percent of our budget on cheap Wal-Martian imports (food, apparel, household furnishings, and electronics). Housing and health care alone get you to 25 percent.

Finally, "Don't we want a strong dollar?" is a trick question. In this case, a good answer might be, "Why opt for anything? Why not let markets decide?" There's a self-regulating mechanism here that keeps a currency from getting too strong: a country's balance of trade. When it gets too large, traders in currency markets—folks buying and selling dollars, yen, francs, and so on—tend to worry about such imbalances, and that lowers demand for the imbalanced currency, which makes it more competitive, which leads to more balanced trade.

But some of our competitors have been fending off such market adjustments, managing their currencies to stay low in value relative to the dollar. The Chinese do this, and it's one reason why they're flooding us with cheap imports while we're unable to return the favor.[25]

Crunchpoint: A strong dollar helps to keep prices down, but it hurts our manufacturers and contributes to large, growing, and ultimately destructive trade imbalances. By the way, the prices of most of what we buy are set right here, not abroad. We should let markets decide the strength of the dollar, even if it means standing up to some tough competitors.

Economics always seems to assume that more is better than less: more money, more consumption, more investment, more stuff, more, more, more! Is economic analysis fundamentally incompatible with conservation and environmentalism?

In theory, no. In practice, I'm afraid so.

This is an important question, of course, because you can be sure that economists are and will continue to be prominently seated at the table when influential bodies take up these matters. Will they be part of the solution or part of the problem?

My fear is that the analysis of many economists (all not of them, but many of the ones with the clout) will make it harder to take the needed action against global warming—specifically, reducing carbon emissions, widely recognized to be at the source of the problem. The reason comes down to an intersection of two powerful forces: a congenital preference, both in economics and human nature, for growth today versus a less polluted tomorrow, and principle #1, regarding power dynamics.

As the question suggests, "More is better than less" is a fundamental precept of economics, and in this context, that notion puts policies that call for sacrificing today in the interest of a better future at a distinct disadvantage. Whether you're arguing for a carbon tax to reduce emissions, a gas tax, or even better mileage standards, some prominent policymaker backed by a prominent economist is going to accuse you of being antigrowth. And as we've seen all too frequently in recent years, if the question is "Pay now or pay later?" the latter—that is, the later—wins.

That's too bad, because economics should be helpful here. We have pretty rigorous methods for accounting for future costs and ought to be able to use those tools to show that the cost of doing nothing is indeed quite high. Those who have tried to do so, however, have quickly found the big pitfall in real-life economics as it's generally practiced today: We heavily discount the future.[26]

Ask an economist what it would cost to build a structure or implement a policy, and we can usually get you pretty close. We can make defensible guesstimates about future wage and material costs or how many people would benefit from a minimum wage increase. But in order to figure the costs of global warming, we need to know (a) what's the potential damage and (b) how much people value the future—what they would pay today to have a cleaner tomorrow, granting that they may not even be here tomorrow.

This puts us on a collision course with the power principle. It's tough to get to the inconvenient truths regarding the potential damage of inaction when deep-pocketed interests are relentless in their pushback. If you want to swim in these waters, never forget this immortal sentence from Upton Sinclair: "It is difficult to get a man to understand something when his salary depends upon his not understanding it." Junk science and its purveyors appear to be pretty deeply embedded in government. Even the venerable Smithsonian Institution, reacting to fears "that it would anger Congress and the Bush administration," recently altered an exhibition on climate change to inappropriately inject some doubt into the mix.[27]

Then there's the matter of who would pay the price to start dealing with this problem. It is widely recognized that to address global warming calls for a quaint little economic dance called *internalizing the externalities*. An *externality* is a situation where some economic player is not paying for the damaging cost of its actions.[28] The classic example is the polluter—a company that generates damages but usually doesn't pay for them. To the contrary, it hires legal council and a team of economists to insulate it from bearing such costs.

With the political will, we could get past that bevy of bloviators and slap a tax on carbon emissions, ergo internalizing the externality—laying the cost of polluting at the feet of the guilty party. But why haven't we done so, especially given that carbon taxes are by now quite common in Europe?[29]

Because for years, all the signals in this debate were urging us to wholly discount any future costs. Who wanted to face higher taxes or prices (firms would pass some part of these taxes forward to consumers in the form of higher prices) when the weather wasn't even all that bad? Pay no heed to those pointy-headed doomsayers. Gas up that SUV and go have a ball.

Those signals are changing in part because the weather does not appear as benign as all that anymore. There are concrete examples in nature—melting ice floes, upticks in temperature beyond what was initially predicted—that are making more of us willing to intervene sooner than later. This very morning, I had to explain to my kid, who can now read headlines, why, according to a study described in a *New York Times* article titled "Warming Is Seen as Wiping Out Most Polar Bears," the bears will be gone by 2050.[30] Here in the present day, the price of gas is likely headed for unprecedented territory, and that too is getting people's attention, including—discouragingly late in the game—American automakers.

Crunchpoint: Economics has perfectly useful tools to help us evaluate the future costs of environment degradation, and good economic rationales—dealing with the negative externalities—for intervening are well established. But the power principle works against us here, as vested interests and the economists (not to mention the scientists) that they own will make sure we see a lot more of the bad kind of economics than the helpful kind in this area. We're also likely to place too little value on the future—and our own psychology, goosed by the vested interests, makes it tough for us to turn our attention to tackling the problem while there's still time. To make any headway in reducing carbon emissions and global warming, we'll need leaders with the courage and foresight to make the case that sacrifices today are critical to stave off potentially monumental losses tomorrow.

5

The Reconnection Agenda

So, you want to change the world?

Certainly there has been a strong critical strain in much of this book. Yet I've tried to stress the tremendous potential of our economy to lift the living standards of the broad majority. It is well within our means to loosen the squeeze, unpack the crunch, and reconnect the growth of incomes across the income scale to that of productivity growth, and not just for a couple of quarters. This reconnection of growth and shared prosperity needs to be the central goal of economic policy, and each idea below was conceived of (and not necessarily by me) in that spirit.

When choosing the policy ideas proposed here, I've employed one other selection criterion: Each is under discussion in some prominent circles. In the interest of realism, there's nothing too pipe-dreamy here. Of course, that doesn't mean any of these ideas will reach fruition. Making that happen is the subject of the final chapter.

The idea is to outline the framework for the solutions to our most important economic challenges. The devil may be in the details, but my goal here is not to wrestle with Satan (that's my day job). It is to distill these challenges down to the one or two key policy pressure points (PPPs) that form the core of a successful initiative in these various areas. The PPPs are the points that any serious attempt to address the issue must speak to. My hope is that readers can then look for these core themes when policymakers start trotting out ideas.

To this end, I present brief discussion in this format: why, what, and why not. That is, what's the *rationale* for this idea set, what are the PPPs, and what *objections* will surface.

Rationale: Given the centrality of this theme to our discussion, I've got to start here, but everything that follows feeds into this one. Implement health care reform in the spirit discussed below, and you've just improved the quality of jobs for tens of millions in our workforce who constantly deal with the inequities and insecurities of the current system.

In sifting through the questions people asked me for this book and elsewhere in my travels, I believe the rationale can be reduced to this: There is a sense among many (I'd say most) working families from the lower to the upper-middle reaches of the income scale that our economic system has subtly tilted against them in a way that it didn't in earlier years.

It's not that they're all falling behind in a dramatic fashion—not at all. Many recognize that they're getting ahead. But the pace of economic advance is slower, the hills are steeper, and the potholes are deeper. The data back this up (see Figure 2.2 in Chapter 2); the real income of the typical, or median, family has grown at a far slower pace—one-fourth as fast, to be precise—over the past few decades than in the prior period (1947 to 1979: 2.5 percent per year; 1979 to 2006: 0.5 percent per year). But I don't imagine that many people—and I include myself, the person who just made the calculation—would either recognize or know what to make of such historical comparisons as they go through their daily lives.

We do, however, know what to make of what we relentlessly see and hear regarding the economy in which we're trying to make ends meet, week in and week out. And that comes down to this: Given the ebullience of the economic elite cheerleading squad, the astronomical wealth returns to the richest of the rich, and the impressive scorecard of the big macro variables discussed earlier, it shouldn't be such a bear to get by. If everything is so freakin' wonderful, why, many of us would like to know, are my children taking on huge debt burdens to get an education, why is a decent home in a neighborhood with a good school slipping from my grasp, and why is my paycheck increasingly squeezed at the pump, the grocery, and the doctor's office?

These are the questions behind the crunch, and they are the targets of the policy set that follows.

PPPs: Though these issues are typically cast as wrenchingly complex, cooking up the corrective policy set is really quite simple. Yes, the punditry, myself included, plays symphonies of chin music around this theme, but let us cut through all of that to the most important reason for the crunch as we know it today: **bargaining power.** Specifically, it's the lack thereof—the difficulty that too many of us have claiming our fair slice of the growing economic pie. I've referred to this throughout as principle #1, and it wasn't for nothing that I gave this concept such primacy. I did so knowing that lots of people want to say the problem isn't power, it's the lack of skills to successfully compete in the new, global economy. As I've stressed throughout, and as I reiterate below under *objections,* skills loom large in my thinking, too—I'm still a card-carrying economist. But they—or, more precisely, their alleged deficits—don't explain the crunch.

So how do you boost bargaining power? Or to be more specific, how do you distribute it more broadly from its currently concentrated position at the top of the wealth scale? Let me count the ways.

First, there's **full employment.** It's an old Keynesian concept that a few economists and even a few politicians are trying to revive.[1] To be more accurate, economists of all stripes talk about the concept of truly tight job markets, but few appreciate the role of full employment in boosting bargaining power and reconnecting growth and broad prosperity. To the contrary, as I pointed out in Chapter 2, most of them deeply fret over the extent to which tight job markets will kick up inflation.

Their priorities are misplaced, and these critically important relationships are poorly understood by powerful people wielding powerful tools. Even as I write today, the unemployment rate, hovering between 4 and 5 percent, is below the rate that economists consider full employment, yet wages and inflation have been on the wane. The absence of full employment is one big reason for the squeeze.

How to get there? The **Federal Reserve**, as discussed in Chapter 3, plays a major role, and even recent history has shown that one thing it can do is move the unemployment rate. That's not a precise calibration, but interestingly, inflation is now more a function of commodity prices set in the world markets, meaning the Fed's main target—inflation—is less under its control. We'd all be better off if it focused more on keeping job growth as robust as possible.[2]

But even a strong macro-tide will leave some disadvantaged workers stranded on the beach. For these folks, connections to the job market will need to be made directly, through the creation of **public service jobs**—jobs created by the public sector to do stuff we need done in the public sector, like fixing roads, bridges, and parks, for starters. I know there are details—you've got to work with the public service unions on this one, as they might well begrudge the competition—but I've looked into it, and these issues can be worked out.[3]

Speaking of **unions**, they're another bargaining power booster. People often think of unionism as doomed due to the demise of manufacturing (which, as discussed below under "Globalization," is another squeeze factor), but the loss of factory jobs explains only one-fifth of the tumble in union membership, from close to 40 percent of the private workforce in the 1950s to 8 percent in the mid-2000s. The rest has come from years of union disinterest in serious organizing. Now that the unions are back in the business of building membership, especially in the service sector, they are faced with the much more important factor of powerful (there's that *power* word again), organized opposition.

Some members of Congress are aware of this problem and they have been tossing around a piece of legislation called the Employee Free Choice Act, aimed at achieving a more balanced playing field for union organizing. It's a good bill that just needs a little tweaking.[4] All the Democrat frontrunners support the bill, so depending on the outcome of the 2008 presidential election, the bill might have some legs.

There are other things we could do to boost bargaining power. **Higher minimum wages** help to compensate for the fact that low-wage workers have the least clout and no real lobby to advocate for them. **Less porous**

safety nets, like an unemployment insurance system that catches more of those who fall out of the job market, are also part of the solution. But as I noted, all of what follows speaks to loosening the squeeze.

How do I know this stuff will work? Full employment, unions, and minimum wages have been shown not only to raise wages, but to raise them most for folks at the bottom of the scale. Refer back to the downward staircase of the bars in Figure 3.1; they show that low-wage workers get the biggest boost from low unemployment. Unions raise wages close to three times more for low-wage workers compared with high-wage workers,[5] and minimum wages by definition go to the lowest-wage workers. The creation of public sector jobs is more dicey—it can be expensive, and it's got a mixed record. So you move slowly, starting out with some local demonstration projects to test the water.

Objections: There are many objections to the above agenda, but I'd say they're all pretty minor. Employer lobbies insist, against the evidence, that moderate minimum wage increases will bring the economy to its knees (see Chapter 2); and lots of economists still tilt more against inflation than toward full employment.

But the two big roadblocks we face here are (a) too few highly placed people understand that the lack of bargaining power is at the heart of the problem, and (b) those that got it are not anxious to share it.

As I've noted throughout, the most common explanation for inequality, the squeeze, and stagnant income growth is a mismatch between skills and the demands of the global economy. Of course, skills and education matter a lot, and the income premium—the wage advantage to highly educated workers relative to those with lower schooling levels—is higher than ever. But one reason it's so high is not that employers have been raising the pay of skilled workers; it's that weak job markets, falling minimum wages, declining unions, trade deficits, manufacturing-job losses, and now the offshoring of white-collar jobs have hacked away at the real earnings of workers across the wage scale. At the same time, those who enter the game with some serious assets and the acumen to play in global financial markets have been absorbing the lion's share of the wealth created by the new economy.

In this context, sticking with skills as the sole explanation constitutes a costly misdiagnosis. As I describe, access to higher education is critically important, but it won't scratch the inequality itch. For that, we need to take steps that go beyond blaming the victim—"If only you were smarter, were better trained, had more credentials . . . all would be yours"—to looking at the structure of power and figuring out how to alter it with the goal of greater equity.

I don't expect those in control to share the reins without a fight. To date, their argument has been an economic one: In our meritocracy, unbiased market forces are the sole and primary arbiters of the distribution of wealth, and such forces should not be tampered with. Unless they're reading this book, and I'll discount that probability, they're blissfully and willfully unaware of the power principles at play.

Our job is to introduce them to precisely these ideas.

HEALTH CARE

Rationale: Once again, it's easy, and ultimately necessary, to make this complicated. There are trillions of dollars at stake, deep-pocketed vested interests, and many different levels of need—and let's not forget that we're talking about a fundamental matter of quality of life here. But, as with immigration, the current path is not sustainable. If we keep climbing the path we're on, we will fairly soon be devoting such a large share of our economy to health care that there won't be enough left over for other stuff we need and care about.

And remember, this is ultimately as much a private sector as public sector matter. Policymakers often discuss the issue in terms of publicly provided health care, like Medicare, becoming too expensive, but that's wrong. Medical spending, regardless of its source, is rising a lot faster than growth in the rest of the economy (in fact, Medicare traditionally controls costs better than private insurance).

The fact that we're not quite there—health care hasn't started crowding out everything else yet—makes it harder to motivate reform. Immigration, education, and global warming seem much more urgent. So one challenge here is getting people interested in big health care regime changes before our fiscal blood pressure goes through the roof. We've got to get the patient to start taking care of herself before she's a basket case.

PPPs: Let's keep it simple by identifying two key pressure points—**pooling risk** and **cutting costs**. The first is easier than the second, but both are absolutely necessary.

I discussed both of these in response to the Chapter 1 question about how we spend our health care dollars a lot less efficiently than other countries, so I'll summarize here. "Everybody in the risk pool" is the clarion call of universal programs, because they spread the likelihood and expense of illness over large groups, and that lowers costs. They also tend to take for-profit, competitive insurers out of the picture, and that too saves big money.

But the real money is in the excesses and inefficiencies of the medical industrial complex. Big Pharma wastes billions on leisure and "me-too" drugs—for example, another blood pressure med that's got some almost useless tweak compared with the last one on the market, or another pill to keep old guys active in bed. Author Maggie Mahar, who has scrutinized these excesses, writes of unnecessary angioplasties and bypass surgeries, second and third rounds of chemo, and other unnecessary tests and treatments, all of which are more likely to diminish a patient's quality of life than to improve it.[6]

The research community is on the take, or at least stuck in the cycle churning out the drugs that generate the highest profit margins, as opposed to ones that will give society the biggest bang for the buck. As Mahar writes, "Patients aren't clamoring for these treatments—they're simply doing what a doctor or hospital tells them they must do." The supplier tells patients what they need, and they're in no position to raise questions.

Consumers tend not to face the costs, so we're usually going to do what the doc tells us, including switching to the marginally useful new pill that she endorses, perhaps because she helped to develop it or spent the weekend golfing with the drug rep. Other than insurers, who make money by getting between people and the care they believe they need, there's no rational watchdog mechanism to reel in this endless, expensive dance between the corporate, research, and medical delivery sectors.

That's how it works for the insured. For the uninsured, as Nobel laureate Joe Stiglitz puts it, "The poor can't pay for drugs, so there is little research on their diseases."[7] And from a cost-savings perspective, applying the prevention lessons we already know would beyond a doubt be even more important than new research. The way things are set up, there's no money in prevention programs aimed at chronic, expensive conditions like high blood pressure, diabetes, and obesity.

Given all this, we shouldn't be surprised that there's little correlation between spending and outcomes. Yet there exists no independent agency for comparative analysis of treatment effectiveness that could help to promote investment into worthwhile areas from the perspective of the public good (most new health plans, at least the ones from Democrats, propose the creation of such an entity).

Objections: Go after the private insurers or try to regulate Big Pharma and you will be accused of thwarting the invisible hand, crushing the competitive spirit, and leading us toward "European-style socialized medicine." This last is just name-calling, and I've already shown that they spend less per capita with better outcomes, on average. But the other charges are serious.

You can imagine, for example, that competition between for-profit drug producers does lead to healthy competition, generating more and better choices. The problem is, it doesn't. There is little relationship between spending, innovation, profits, and medical breakthroughs.

Why? Because markets tend to be fairly lousy at providing public goods, and as much as we want to think otherwise, medicine ultimately fits under that heading. I would no more want the government in the iPod business than I'd want private drug companies to prioritize what's important (they're likely to stress erectile dysfunction over chronic asthma). Then there's the fact that the patent system in medicine ranges from inefficient to lethal: In the interest of protecting profits, patents work as an exclusivity license to keep prices of drugs and treatments out of reach for many who need them. The result is that sick people without resources, both here and abroad, don't benefit from medical breakthroughs. And, as noted, there's no real price mechanism at the end of the line: The insured don't have much incentive to question why their MD is telling them to get that test or switch to that new med, and the uninsured aren't even in the game.

So we're left with all the classic symptoms of a market failure: few price signals, lack of information (most of us don't have the needed info to evaluate what the docs tell us), and heaps of negative externalities.

When markets fail, even conservative economists recognize a role for government. Our best move at this point would be to move to a universal system and phase the private insurers out of the picture, or at least change their incentives so that they're not in the business of denying care to those need it. However, many in the front lines of this movement tell me that the $700 billion insurance industry is not going gently into that good night. So here's the plan.

We need to set up competing systems: private versus public, touch gloves, come out fighting, may the best man win. That is, craft a set of rules regarding the playing field to avoid cheating—straightforward stuff like everybody's got to be covered and every health care plan has to meet a basic standard. To help with cost control and the identification of what works best, get truly independent evaluation panels up and running (it will take some serious oversight to keep the foxes out of this henhouse), and get them feeding their "better bang for the buck" results to an expanded National Institutes of Health, the federal government's highly successful medical research unit, which in turn informs the insurers, public and private, of its findings.

Allow people (or employers who purchase coverage for their staff members) the choice of going with private coverage or a public program, likely something in the spirit of Medicare for All. Then kick back and see who is best able to effectively achieve the dual goals of full coverage and cost containment. My money's on the public system, but I'm ready to be surprised.

There are a few plans much like this, and for those of you who like details or are having trouble sleeping, they're worth a close look.[8]

Before I leave this topic, there's another potential objection worth exploring. We may soon be asking people, many of whom are relatively contented with their health care plans (though I'm sure this number is shrinking), to try a very different approach to health care, one that may not involve markets, employers, and private insurers. Why should they change? What's in it for them?

In some cases, we may be asking for personal sacrifices. Most of the health care plans I've seen call for greater spending through the tax system. That is, while these plans save money by tapping efficiencies that are currently eluding us big time, we are likely to shift from private sector to greater public sector expenditures; and while many people's medical spending will go down, some people's taxes will rise to fit the bill.

All of which reminds me of a scene in Michael Moore's interesting commentary on comparative health care systems, *SiCKO*. Moore visits a Canadian man who was injured playing golf and asks him why he—Moore or any other person—should have to pay for someone else's misfortune or destructive choices. "Because I'd do the same for you," the man replies.

What I take from that exchange is that the motivation for tackling this particular challenge will need to come from the realization that we're all in this together. We've been fed a very divisive political gruel for the past few decades, and it has served to empower many mean-spirited, greedy people. They have revealed themselves to be incapable of recognizing that some problems—and health care is the best example—are more efficiently solved by collective cooperation than by individuals competing. The glaring failures of their "You're on your own" philosophy are becoming clear in many areas of our political life, from Middle East policy to taxes, globalization, and health care. With that, their influence appears to be waning.

It will take some incisive, inspired leadership to clear the damage and help set out a new path. The good news is that on this issue of health care, I see precisely these actions being taken by a variety of highly placed political actors, from most of the front-runners in the '08 presidential election, and not just the Democrats.[9] Of course, the last time we tried this was with the Bill Clinton national health care plan. We got nowhere, but that was a far too complicated plan that misfired on both PPPs (there was some risk pooling and cost cutting, but not nearly enough); and, just as important, times have changed. With the right plan, strategy (see the next chapter), and leadership, reform could be within our reach.

IMMIGRATION

Rationale: As the latest round of immigration reform (2006-07) has clearly shown, this is one tough issue. Though polls (that's *polls* with an s—I'm not cherry-picking my favorite one) show that significant majorities support a welcoming version of reform,[10] there is a small but influential and loud opposition movement favoring a much more restrictive approach to immigration than what has prevailed for the past generation. Yet, while there have been many ugly chapters in our immigration history and periods when native-born workers have fought against immigrant labor, the overarching story is one of successful economic integration.

That is the key to the policy. As I noted in Chapter 4, the problem is not immigration but *illegal* immigration, the loss of border control, and the creation of a permanent underclass of workers and families who are by definition blocked from integrating into the mainstream. A closely related problem is that a large and powerful lobby of low-wage employers has become addicted to an unending flow of cheap labor supply. These are the pressure points of a successful policy set.

PPPs: Thus, the two goals of immigration policy, in order—and the order is very important—must be **control of immigrant flows** and **economic integration**. We cannot reform our broken system unless we can prohibit illegal flows. There are only two ways to do this: make them legal—open the borders—or create a system that identifies illegal workers and penalizes employers for hiring them. Yes, I've omitted the wall option because I don't think it will work; and it seems wrong and offensive, and sends precisely the wrong message in a globalizing economy.

The first option, open borders, would likely engender large and daunting changes to our national identity, and it is not something that we or any other advanced economy would realistically consider. So the second option is where policy needs to head. A **nationalized identity system** may sound Big Brotherish or worse ("Show me your papers . . . where are your papers?!"), but there's no way around it. You need to identify yourself to fly in an airplane, and sooner rather than later, you'll probably need to do so to work too.

Once we get this process under way, we can turn to **earned citizenship** for those already here. For all the opposition that idea gets, from the perspective of policy that generates the best outcomes for the most people, it's pretty much a no-brainer. It helps the undocumented by bringing them out of the shadow economy and into the real one, and it helps those native workers with whom they compete, since the formerly undocumented workers are less likely to face workplace exploitation (meaning native workers' wages won't be undercut). And it supports what has to be one of society's primary goals: the integration of these families into the mainstream.

There is a final PPP here, one I referenced earlier in Chapter 4: This debate needs a little more empathy/sympathy for those who oppose a more welcoming version of immigration reform. I'm not talking about the racists who want to keep people who look different from themselves away from our shores, and I'm not talking about TV opportunists who are stoking the fires of xenophobia and hatred.

I'm talking about people who have been, or believe they have been, hurt by immigrant competition. To deny their experience, or to argue that the impact is "economically small" or merely a "transitional cost," is a recipe for cooking up ever-greater resistance to needed reforms. Instead, their plight—perhaps it's your plight—needs to be acknowledged and recognized in the context of the crunch that I've tried to articulate in these pages. There really are families whose living standards have been diminished by immigrant competition. In fact, some of these families are members of older immigrant cohorts themselves. The way forward is to craft an immigration policy that is fair and welcoming to those who want to come here legally, while we simultaneously craft an economic agenda that reconnects all working families to the growing economy.

Objections: The main objection to citizenship for undocumented immigrants is that it sends a message to those considering illegal immigration to "come on up." In fact, some research suggests that's what happened after the last round of reforms in the mid-1980s. The reason, though, was that we never undertook step one: **control the flows.** We had neither the commitment nor the technology. If we repeat the failure, there will be no reform. And without reform, I fear our dysfunctional immigration system will collapse in a manner that could turn dangerous and violent.

EDUCATION

Rationale: There are so many reasons for getting this right—for making sure the system is truly working to ensure that all comers reach their potential—that I hardly need to give a rationale for its inclusion as a policy priority. In fact, it's important to pare down the question to manageable proportions. In the context of our discussion, there are two dimensions of education policy to consider. First, how can we harness education to reduce growing inequalities; second, what needs to be done to loosen the squeeze associated with paying for college?

PPPs: The experts speak to many PPPs, some truly important (class size), some largely ideologically driven (injecting market competition into the public school system). As regards the two contextual points above, the key pressure points are (a) **offset the inequalities at the starting gate,** and (b) couple **access to higher ed with remediation** for anyone motivated enough to go.

As the work of education policy guru Richard Rothstein has shown, we can't ask education to offset the economy's inequalities when the system itself is laden with the damaging consequences of those inequities.[11] Or, to put it another way, the economists have it backward: It's not that education is driving inequality outcomes; it's that inequality is driving educational outcomes. There are many great studies I could cite, like the ones that show how economically stressed families simply spend less time talking to or preparing their preschoolers for learning, or show the education deficits that are driven by inadequate health, dental, and vision care.[12] But I trust I can assert this.

The beauty part is that you can address a couple of different issues with one narrow policy thrust. Again, organize health care to promote universal access and you've scored here as well. Hit full employment and you've boosted the earning power of disadvantaged families whose kids need parents with good, steady jobs.

Under this framework, policymakers lose points—a lot of points—by bashing the education system for problems it neither created nor can solve. When someone tells you they want to cut taxes on "investors" (code: those in the top tax bracket), privatize health care, screw unions, oppose minimum wages, and "fix the schools," be aware that it doesn't work that way. It's all connected, man.

The next PPP comes from research that shows the following: College-completion rates are about the same for smart, poor kids as they are for—hmmm . . . how shall I put it?—less-than-smart rich kids. About a third of low-income kids with test scores in the top tier complete college. That's about the same share for rich kids with low test scores.[13] Again, I suspect I don't need a lot of research to drive this point home. While it's true that few even upper-income kids pay the sticker price for college, the real costs of tuition have been surpassing income growth, and that's *average* income growth. For those at the low end, college is increasingly out of reach. This, as much as any problem I've raised in this book, is a pure violation of what we ought to be about in America. As a result, college-completion rates are now rising considerably more slowly than they did even in recent years.

The answer is to facilitate college admission and completion for anyone, and I mean anyone, willing and able. Both—admission and completion—are important, but we've been slow to recognize the latter. Enrollment rates among minorities, for example, have grown considerably faster than completion rates. The reason is that once they get there, many children from disadvantaged backgrounds are hard-pressed to make it through.

A good example of this problem in action is a policy I always thought was exactly the ticket: the top 10 percent rule. Under this plan, implemented by a few states, including Texas under Governor George W. Bush, if you perform in the top 10 percent in your high school, you're automatically admitted to a public college (most states provide significant help to foot the bill). Now, based on the inequalities discussed above, your high school could be severely disadvantaged, meaning that, measured against all the students in your community, you might be well below the top decile.

But no matter. The beauty of the top 10 percent rule is that as long as you've shown yourself to be a top *relative* performer—relative to your peers in your school—you're in.

However, what we've found, unsurprisingly, is that many of these kids need remediation and income support. It's not enough to give them a congratulatory slap on the back as you drop them off curbside at State U. Again, the fact that they excelled in their schools tells you something important about them: They've prevailed against adversity. It tells you little about their actual levels of preparedness. At any rate, with consistent support, this seems like a manageable, fixable problem.

Objections: Like I said, there are those that blame the schools, and their solutions tend to be less about going after the roots of the problems, as I've suggested above, and more about restructuring the system. Most favor some form of privatization, and most believe that teachers' unions are a big part of the problem.

While many folks who view these issues through the same lens as I oppose these measures, I take a different tack. I'm entirely open to the idea that public schools are unresponsive to market discipline that could make them more responsive to legitimate concerns. And, particularly in minority communities, parents have made the argument to me, "There are schools in my community that you wouldn't send your kids to in a million years." They're right. I am not going to defend the status quo to these parents.

The problem is, as with health care, market concepts somehow map in surprisingly ineffective ways onto public goods. Markets kick butt when you need to accurately price pork bellies. But they don't work here. Just think about one of our most beloved economic concepts: productivity growth. Is a teacher more productive when she adds 10 students to the class? In fact, she's probably less so, but our measures can't capture that.

In practice, charter schools—public schools with charters that free them from local requirements, including union rules—have produced no better student outcomes than regular public schools, which is one of the reasons why I'm sure the inequality point is such a strong one.[14] These kids are going to schools with disadvantages bequeathed to them by our ever-more-inequitable society, and that's where we've got to meet this problem.

GLOBALIZATION

Rationale: It's big, it's bad, it's great, it's here to stay, and we'd better start dealing with it.

We're not yet doing so—dealing with it, that is. The YOYOs (the "You're on your own" squad) I discussed back in Chapter 3 argue that expanded trade relations, more immigration, and the increased speed at which people, ideas, and money can zip around the globe is a benign force that is already enriching us far more than we realize. They've had to acknowledge the turbulence therein, but they write this off to transition costs that can't be avoided, or at least not without killing the golden goose.

The ironic thing is that they're undermining their case. As I stressed in Chapter 4, the majority of the public is increasingly out of sync with this Panglossian view. In the few polls that have looked at this, there seems to be a nuanced understanding among the majority that expanded trade is good for the economy but it's not good for them, and this hits right at the heart of the reconnection agenda.

So here I am, coming to the aid of the same free-traders who usually don't want me to play in their sandbox. It's OK, guys—I'm happy to help think about ways we can make this work for people.

PPPs: The things people worry most about concerning globalization, and I'm talking about both blue- and white-collar workers, are job security and quality, the latter referring to wages and compensation. How can we maintain our lifestyles if we're in direct competition with those who can do what we do for a lot less? And don't think you'll assuage anybody with claptrap about lower-priced goods. People who are worried about their jobs, their living standards, and especially their kids' prospects are not amused by stories of cheap socks.

Nor, as discussed above, do they believe that more education is the sole answer. Much to our surprise, we've learned in recent years that people in India and China have brains, too, and while these countries do not yet have the resources to provide higher education to large shares of their populations, those populations are so large that even small shares are hugely boosting the global supply of skill along with their comparative advantage (which in China's case is, of course, abundant, cheap labor). Under current trends, by 2010, China will graduate more PhDs in science and engineering than the United States.

So any globalization agenda needs to address this issue of **job security and quality.** There are two good ways to do so. We can soften the blow by providing more extensive social insurance, or we can try to create more opportunity. The latter idea, which is far more radical (and admittedly departs a bit from my pledge to stick to ideas that are actively in the mix with top policy players), is best discussed in economese. Globalization raises the supply of labor; we need to raise the domestic demand to offset the supply shift.

Note that I do not entertain protectionist ideas. Globalization is a juggernaut that can be shaped, not stopped. Its benefits should be tapped and enhanced, and its costs recognized and treated. As discussed in Chapter 4, I do believe we should craft trade agreements that boost the bargaining power of workers here and abroad. Predictably, these have been opposed by the investor class, whose interests have been amply represented in such deals thus far, so some pushback here is due. But while we fight about that stuff a lot in DC, I don't consider tweaks to trade agreements real PPPs. They're too indirect.

Let us take some of the benefits of trade and plow them into **universal health care** and **pensions**, two systems of critical importance that employers cannot be counted upon to maintain, particularly given the heightened competitiveness that globalization engenders. But let's not stop there.

Replacing some of the labor demand that globalization zaps is the more ambitious part of the agenda. The **full-employment** ideas discussed above travel well to the globalization debate, but here are two cross-cutting ideas that are starting to get some attention: initiate an ambitious, public/private drive for **energy independence**, and invest deeply in **public infrastructure**.

The water for the first idea is being carried by the Apollo Alliance, a really interesting group of disparate folks who have given the most thought to creating an energy-independence agenda.[15] Their motto says it quite succinctly: "Three Million New Jobs, Independence from Foreign Oil." Who could be against that?

I'm not naive, and surely the path of history is littered with failed initiatives to achieve energy independence. But in this context, I'm not going to argue these points or question whether that three million number is accurate. The point is that we need to get outside the passive box that views globalization as "happening to us" and aggressively seek ways to deal with its downsides. The Apollo Alliance is a solution to two huge challenges: our unsustainable dependence on fossil fuels, as well as diminished domestic demand for workers across the educational scale. It's worth a close look.

In the same vein, we should also consider the fact that civil engineers tell us there is a deficit worth more than $1 trillion in our public infrastructure—the roads, bridges, airports, sewers, schools, communication systems, and more that play such a critical role in our nation's productive capacity. Private markets fail to address these deficits, because they are generally unable to capture the economic benefits of doing so. So here's another twofer: public investment and quality job creation. It ain't free, and I address costs at the end of this chapter.

Objections: The squawking you hear around globalization tends to be triggered more by perceived protectionist measures than by ideas like those above. Of course, the YOYO society will object to safety nets in the form of both greater social insurance and direct job creation, although invoking market failure might even get some of those folks on board (that is, markets have thus far been unresponsive to the need for energy independence, and they will, by definition, underinvest in public infrastructure).

But you need a more-robust, better-run, and better-endowed public sector to pull off this stuff. We can't meet the challenges of globalization with a diminished presence for the federal government. As with health care, this is a "We're in this together" moment. Atlas may have been able to hold the globe on his shoulders, but as for the rest of us, we can't tackle globalization on our own.

WHAT'S LEFT?

There are a lot of big challenges I haven't touched upon, most notably global warming. As I pointed out in Chapter 4, I fear economists are not going to lead the way on this one, so I'm less prone to include it in my list. Also, while it's at the top of my personal list of concerns, it's broader than the reconnection agenda. We can implement all the best ideas in the world regarding full employment and globalization, but if we're beset by rising sea levels, vicious weather patterns, and polluted natural resources, our best will be for naught.

I also haven't spoken to one of my favorite policy topics: poverty in America. That's because I believe poverty these days is largely driven by precisely the same force I've addressed above: the split between overall growth and the living standards of the broad majority. In fact, research has shown that if the relationship between poverty and growth remained much the same as in the pre-inequality era (prior to the 1980s), poverty rates would be minuscule. Instead, we've made almost no progress since the late 1970s.

As pointed out in Chapter 1, poverty rates fell sharply in the latter 1990s during a short full-employment period when the benefits of productivity growth were broadly shared. But in the absence of full employment, they rose again through the mid-2000s, despite the acceleration of productivity. So I'm convinced that the agenda outlined is also the right one for the reduction of poverty amid plenty.

Let me slip in one more little idea, which, you may be surprised to learn, keeps to my promise to stick to ideas that have some traction in high places. We should set a poverty target. That is, we should set a goal to have our poverty rate, or maybe our child poverty rate, down to some low level by some given date. I know it sounds gimmicky, and it is, but believe me, a hard-nosed wonk like yours truly wouldn't even go there if I hadn't seen it work with my own eyes.

The Blair government in the UK set a target of ending child poverty by 2020, with various interim targets along the way. To an American, this may seem a little nuts: Why give your opponent something to fry you with if you miss the target? But the way it played out in the UK was quite different. It clearly focused the minds of policymakers, who rolled up their sleeves and got to work on the issue, and the results were dramatic.[16] Though they missed the first ambitious step of lowering child poverty by a quarter, they did get it down by 17 percent. Over that same period through the first half of the 2000s, U.S. child poverty was up by 13 percent, despite productivity growth that surpassed that of the UK.

You want to know why the Apollo Alliance took that name? Because when President Kennedy announced the Apollo moon shot program, he had no idea how the goal of landing someone on the moon in 10 years would be achieved. Neither does the Alliance know how or if we can achieve energy independence in a decade. But without a target, we're more likely to slog along with no motivating benchmarks against which to measure our progress. The fact that for the first time in our history of tracking the poor, poverty rates rose for the first three years of an economic recovery should be the kick in the pants we need to recognize a good idea whose time has come.[17]

Now, you'll have noticed I said nothing about how much any of this will cost. That's because (a) you can't cost out ideas at this level of vagueness, and (b) you wouldn't want to, beyond rough estimates, even if you could. The minute you attach a price tag, someone's going to say you can't afford it; and now that you've read Chapter 3, that should make you as mad as it does me, and I'm trying to stay calm here. But go ahead, make my day: Explain to me why we can afford wars and tax cuts but not poverty targets.

Full employment is actually a moneymaker, so that one's easy. If we are below our potential in terms of labor market tautness, we're losing national income, including government revenue (that is, we're sacrificing potential growth of jobs, incomes, and tax revenue). The big-ticket item is health care reform.

How much will that cost? Well, keep in mind that on net, any plan that adheres to the PPPs above will save money, relative to the $2.2 trillion current system. But let's not be too cute. The good, new plans will also raise the public sector's share of the costs now being expended. How much depends on how you go about it. Here, like anywhere else in life, you get what you pay for.

Plans such as those touted by 2008 Democratic presidential candidates Hillary Clinton, Barack Obama, and John Edwards—plans that adhere to the PPPs above—cost the federal government something like $50 billion to $100 billion per year (Edwards' and Clinton's plans adhere more closely, and thus their costs come in at the higher end of this range). All three plans, however, make a strong case for savings that exceed these costs. Cost estimates for extending Medicare down the age scale, or Medicare for All, another good idea for universal coverage, are also in the $100 billion range, at least once you factor in the savings from implementing some of the ideas discussed above.

If we were at the beginning of this book instead of at the end, I'd shyly defend such spending as a worthwhile endeavor that amounts to a few percent of GDP in the interest of taking a basic human right out of the marketplace, where it is currently inequitably and highly inefficiently delivered to those with the resources while denied to those without. Now, I can proudly and loudly proclaim that significant investment in progressive health care reform is a *crunchpoint* priority.

In fact, every idea I've espoused in this book fits into a plausible, doable, and not-at-all radical agenda intended to promote a new vision of our economy. Each case balances the needs and wants of the broad swath of working families with my desire to preserve and promote the free-market forces that make our economy so dynamic and productive. That balance is sorely lacking in our current economy. Anyone looking for your vote who neither recognizes our current imbalances nor proposes to address them doesn't deserve it.

Oh dear, I seem to have stumbled from policy into politics. As you see, we've got good ideas. And with that, we come to our next big question: What needs to happen for these and any other good ideas to move off these pages and into our economic lives? Read on.

Conclusion:
The Lesson of the Rink

IF YOU WANT SOMETHING DONE RIGHT . . .

My last book, *All Together Now: Common Sense for a Fair Economy*, presented a broad vision of where economic policy has gotten off track and where it should be headed. When I made this argument to people, someone would invariably raise the question, "What can we do to see that ideas like these have a chance to get implemented?"

This is, of course, a fundamental question, but one I hadn't thought enough about. Back then, I viewed my job as crunching the numbers, communicating the story they told, and helping build the policy agenda to get those numbers moving back in the right direction. I lazily figured that someone else could do the heavy lifting to translate the ideas (not necessarily my ideas, but any good ideas along the same lines) into action.

I no longer see it that way. True, much of what we've discussed in this book is explanatory material that hopefully helps to make sense of the economics debate swirling around us. But there's also an agenda embedded in all this, as the previous chapter showed. It includes a more activist approach to meeting the challenges we face, from globalization to health care to inequality.

The question is, how do you get there from here? Of course, that's partly, if not largely, a political question, and I take great solace in the fact that leading presidential candidates are discussing these issues, sometimes with considerable insight. As noted in the last chapter, all the Democratic frontrunners in the 2008 presidential election posted scads of pages on their campaigns' Web sites explaining the nooks and crannies of their health care plans (clearly they're ignoring the campaign adage, go detailed too early, and the forces of darkness will be all over you before you can say "Swift boat"). Presidential elections aside, the question becomes, what will it take for the majority of the electorate to get behind a progressive economic agenda? That is, not just to vote for candidates who say they'll do the right thing, but to stay focused on those candidates and the political process until they follow through.

THE LESSON OF THE RINK

Like I said, I gave short shrift to that question in my last book and did not want to repeat that mistake here. So, one Saturday last winter, I sat staring at a blank computer screen, randomly pecking out disconnected thoughts, ultimately squandering a precious hour before I had to take my seven-year-old daughter to an ice skating party.

Once we got to the rink, I parked myself at the side, enjoying the crisp, sunny afternoon and watching the kids figure out how to skate. In the back of my mind, though, I was still mulling over this question of what it would take to shift the debate, to motivate both policymakers and their true clients—the electorate—to recognize the need to solve the economic challenges we face with policies like those discussed in the last chapter.

Then I noticed something peculiar. All of a sudden—at least it seemed sudden—the skaters were all going around in the opposite direction. That is, after the hourly break when the ice was cleaned, the skaters had started out going around to the right. Now they were circling left. Right to left . . . hmmm . . . wasn't that exactly what I was looking for?

I immediately set to figuring out how this occurred, to see if it was transferable to the world beyond the ice. During the next session, they never switched, but in the last session before the birthday cake, the skaters again switched direction, and this is how it happened.

The main body of skaters, most of whom were pretty shaky on their skates, stayed close to the edge of the rink and went around in the direction they started out in. But as the session went on, a group of skaters, typically ones that were pretty skilled and didn't need to hug the fence, skated much closer to the middle of the ice.

Now, in the center of the ice rink, the circle is much smaller, and as these kids fooled around, doing little spins and jumps and whatnot, their little circles wouldn't always end up going in the same direction as the masses. The next thing I knew, skaters who were in between the fence and the group in the middle of the ice started going in the same direction as the group in the center, which was now established as different from the group on the fence. Finally, the fence skaters would sense that they were out of sync with the other skaters, and they too would shift direction.

Aha, I thought, a change in direction has to emanate from independent thinkers in the center. Here in DC, where I ply my trade, we often disparage centrists as muddled wishy-washers who can't make up their minds and "triangulate" themselves into meaningless positions. And there are those who clearly do so.

But the lesson of the skating rink is that a change in direction rarely comes from the majority skating along at the outer edges of the rink. Barring a big event—an announcement from the folks running the rink, a huge macroeconomic shock—they won't shift direction, because from where they sit, or skate, it's a very big deal to turn around the other way. But for those in the middle of the ice, the difference between going one way and going the other is small.

A SUGAR RUSH?

I know . . . you're thinking I had one too many cupcakes, but let me try to explain how this maps onto a progressive policy agenda. From the top, the leader who will introduce the ideas that meet the challenges we face will have to do so from the narrow center, tacking subtly in a new direction.

While I've highlighted many problematic trends, I've also stressed many positive aspects of our economy. Thankfully, this is not the Great Depression, when a huge change in direction was needed for us to regain prosperity. Instead, some of us fall far behind, most muddle through, some do better than that, and a precious few dwell in the economic stratosphere (I'm told that Microsoft magnate Paul Allen has two big yachts, one of which has a submarine on it—how's that for a spare tire?).

Think of two of our most pressing challenges: our health care system and carbon emissions. Both of these megaproblems are unsustainable: The former threatens to swamp our economy, the latter to do punishing, arguably permanent, damage to the environment. Yet since most of us are still covered by health insurance and can still enjoy a beautiful day, we're unlikely to quickly get behind big changes, like national single-payer health insurance, carbon or gasoline taxes, and a full frontal attack on the medical industrial complex—especially with heavily vested interests fighting to maintain the status quo.

Instead, at least in the near term, and assuming we play our cards right, we're more likely to make little changes that begin to tilt in a new direction—changes that emanate from the middle of the rink. States will experiment with new forms of public health coverage and pollution control. The Feds will extend public health insurance coverage to more groups, like low-income kids. We'll initiate small changes in safety nets; maybe come up with some more subsidized child care slots for working parents or college tuition assistance to loosen the middle-class squeeze.

These are small-bore changes, ones that surely help, but they don't meet the magnitude of the problems we face. They're a few kids trying some new stuff in the center of the ice—they're not a big change in the flow of the traffic.

But it's what happens, or doesn't happen, next that matters.

For major changes to occur—to truly reform our national health care system, to take the necessary steps to rebalance the distribution of wealth and opportunity, to reorganize government spending to most efficiently meet our needs and ensure our safety—these small changes must be met by a public willing to try skating in the other direction.

Above I noted the obvious point that it takes a catastrophe to turn things around. But there are two other conditions wherein large new initiatives come about. In the first case, people aren't paying much attention. In the other, they are.

The best example of the former condition—lack of attention—is the George W. Bush years. The wealthy were already doing extremely well, yet we watched Congress enact large tax cuts that essentially transferred our hard-won budget surplus to the top income classes. And while they were busy playing reverse Robin Hood, they got the country mired in a tragic war, at tremendous cost in life and treasure.

Well, I think it's fair to say that the events I've just described have gotten our attention. The failure of the conservative movement is not just an intellectual phenomenon for DC think tanks to ponder; polling data consistently show it's widely recognized.[1] And note: This is not merely a failure to address challenges. Their sins are of commission, not omission; their actions have exacerbated these challenges, from global warming (anticonservation) to inequality (the Bush tax cuts) to foreign policy (don't get me started . . .).

Thus I conclude that we are in a period in which condition #2 prevails: We are paying attention. That's a very good thing; and given this climate, allow me to close out our discussion by sharing a theory of change—an idea about how change occurs, straight from the ice skating rink at Pentagon Centre, right between the DSW shoe store and the Noodles & Company restaurant (and there must have been a Starbucks there, too).

If the skaters in the middle get too crazy, the rest of us, already shaky on our skates, will get spooked and leave the ice. But if they quietly start skating in the other direction, creating a new momentum, their change will start to reverberate. After all, most of us (consistently around 70 percent by mid-2007—see the previous footnote) think we're headed in the wrong direction. It's just that we've got so much forward momentum that we're hard-pressed to reverse course unless it's a massive, popular shift.

In practical terms, if this change theory is correct, left-leaning centrists may have an edge in this change. We're not ready for a president or Congress to nationalize health care tomorrow, but we are ready for one to plot the course for the next 5 to 10 years to get us there. We're not ready to implement extensive conservation standards, like 40-plus per gallon fuel efficiency tomorrow. But we are ready to start moving in that direction incrementally.

It all probably sounds very unsexy, but I'm a realist. Probably you are, too. If so, you know that when it comes to significant political changes, this is a conservative country, with deep-pocketed vested interests that will fight you tooth and nail every step of the way.

I hate it when politicians talk about "the American people," as if we're monolithic, when we're among the most diverse populations in the world. So forgive me for the broad generalities, but while we may not be very good skaters, we are pragmatic. If we understand what we're up against and are clearly presented with the options, the majority will make the right choices.

Given the opportunity, we will choose to use our vast economic resources to build a better world for our children. We will choose the health care reform that is most efficient and fair. We will choose forward-looking environmental policies that conserve our resources. We will choose to reduce the inequalities that divide us and rob too many of us of our birthright to a fair shake at the dream.

But we've got to know the options. For that to happen, we need two things: politicians who will speak truth to power, and the critical faculty necessary to recognize when we're being snowed. Yes, the former is always in short supply; building up the latter is a prime motivation for this book. If I've done my job, by now you know that when the bigwigs tell you, in the name of sound economic policy, "We can't afford that" and "We can't help with this" and "You'll kill growth if you do that," they must be challenged.

As graduates of Crunch University, you are encouraged to have no patience with those who impatiently and dismissively explain that the invisible hand directing optimal outcomes must not be nudged one way or the other. You must dissent loudly when Wall Street applauds a rising unemployment rate or some economist points out that rich people need tax cuts while poor people need benefit cuts.

Once we truly understand the role that power plays in economics, and how this once-useful tool has been hijacked by those who would use their power to accumulate more resources than could possibly be justified by any sane criterion, we begin to demystify and revitalize economic analysis. My hope is that, as a result of this demystification, we can find the clarity needed to tap the tremendous strength of market forces for the benefit of the majority.

In doing so, we will reinvest the benefits of growth in an architecture that ensures those benefits are broadly shared. Our new agenda, informed by clear-eyed economic analysis that both promotes market forces and pushes back hard against the distortions engendered by excessive greed, power, and wealth concentration, recognizes where markets work and where they fail. And it supports the former by fixing the latter. It takes the necessary steps to shore up the bargaining power of those who are contributing to growth but failing to reap its benefits.

And with that, my farewell crunchpoint:

For too many people, economics has gotten a bad rap. As we established early on, it's nothing more than how we organize our society to provide for our wants and needs. Yet somewhere along the way, it became a tool to explain why we can't organize society in a way that most of us think is fair, equitable, and efficient.

That's changing. The failure and limits of economic policy

as currently practiced are quite glaring. The pervasive and growing inequities we face are quietly, slowly, and perniciously eroding people's support for our system of democracy and free markets. Untreated, they lead to distrust and defunding of government, diminished participation in the political system, protectionism and nativism, and a mean-spiritedness that is as divisive as it is pessimistic.

We all have the tools to treat these cancerous inequities: our minds, our spirits, our sense of community, our concern and love for our children and those of others, our votes. Let's use these tools wisely. Let's use them now.

Notes

PREFACE

1. Since I'm auditioning to be your economic tour guide, some disclosure is in order. I've been employed as an economist since the early 1990s, but my PhD is in social welfare. This means I studied economics through the lens of social policy, which gave me a chance to learn the rules and models of economics along with the real-life impact of those rules once they're implemented.

CHAPTER 1: THE BIG SQUEEZE

1. Source: Economy's growth is measured by real gross domestic product, see http://www.bea.gov/national/nipaweb/Index.asp, table 1.1.6. Real median weekly earnings are for full-time workers, Bureau of Labor Statistics, http://www.bls.gov/cps/cpswktabs.htm, series No. LEU0252881600.

2. Source: U.S. Bureau of the Census, http://www.census.gov/hhes/www/poverty/histpov/hstpov2.html.

3. As discussed later in the text, the median is the 50th percentile, right in the middle of the scale, and "working age" means the household is headed by someone under 65, since older families are much more likely to be retired. See Jared Bernstein, Elise Gould, and Lawrence Mishel, "Income Picture," Economic Policy Institute, August 28, 2007, http://www.epi.org/content.cfm/webfeatures_econindicators_income20070828, for more detail on such income trends.

4. The household income data come from the U.S. Census Bureau; all of these other figures are from the U.S. Bureau of Labor Statistics.

5. Pew Research Center for the People & the Press, *Trends in Political Values and Core Attitudes: 1987–2007—Political Landscape More Favorable to Democrats*, p. 12, http://people-press.org/reports/pdf/312.pdf.

6. Economists talk a lot about productivity growth, and I devote a question to it later, but it's worth briefly describing now: Productivity is how much output (goods and services) we create per hour of work. It's both a measure of the economy's efficiency—if we're creating more stuff in the same number of hours, we're by definition producing more efficiently—and a measure of the wealth that's available to boost our living standards. Now, whether that wealth reaches the people who create it . . . as we shall see, that's another question.

7. Jonathan Weisman, "Snow Concedes Economic Surge Is Not Benefiting People Equally," *Washington Post*, August 9, 2005.

8. The White House, "President Bush Delivers State of the Economy Report," January 31, 2007, http://www.whitehouse.gov/news/releases/2007/01 /20070131-1.html.

9. The White House, "Fact Sheet: October 2007 Marks Record 50th Consecutive Month of Job Growth," http://www.whitehouse.gov/infocus /economy/, accessed November 4, 2007.

10. Between August 2003 and June 2007, employment by the measure used here was up 6 percent. Over the same period in the 1990s recovery, it was up 10 percent, which is about the historical average.

11. The wages here refer to those of the blue-collar workers in manufacturing and non-managers in services, who pretty much make up the bottom 80 percent of the workforce, ranked by wage levels.

12. That's the difference in the averages divided by the number of people, or $(22 - 3)/5$.

13. See Economic Policy Institute, Economic Snapshots, "Recent Income Gains Went to Those with Highest Income," March 28, 2007, http://www.epi.org/content.cfm/webfeatures_snapshots_20070328.

14. John Schmitt, *The Rise in Job Displacement, 1991–2004: The Crisis in American Manufacturing*, http://www.cepr.net/documents/publications/labor _markets_2004_08.pdf.

15. While some argue that the gender gap has now all but closed (see, for example, Carrie Lukas, "A Bargain at 77 Cents to a Dollar," *Washington Post*, April 3, 2007, http://www.washingtonpost.com/wp-dyn/content/article /2007/04/02/AR2007040201262.html?hpid=opinionsbox1), academic research shows that it still exists. At this point, women's earnings are about 75 to 85 percent of those of comparable men.

16. See Lawrence Mishel, Jared Bernstein, and Sylvia Allegretto, *The State of Working America*, 2006/07 edition (Washington, DC: Economic Policy Institute), p. 88, http://www.stateofworkingamerica.org/.

17. Sources: Child care, college tuition, audio equipment, and computers (CPI price data on computers available only since 1998), Bureau of Labor Statistics; median home price, Moody's Economy.com (www.economy.com); health premiums, Kaiser Family Foundation, Employer Health Benefits 2005 Annual Survey, http://www.kff.org/insurance/7315/sections/ehbs05-6-1.cfm.

18. Robin Toner and Janet Elder, "Most Support U.S. Guarantee of Health Care," *New York Times*, March 2, 2007, http://query.nytimes.com/gst /fullpage.html?res=9E06E7D71631F931A35750C0A9619C8B63&sec =health&spon=&pagewanted=2.

19. This certainly describes the Democrats running for president in 2008, and some of the Republicans too. For example, Mitt Romney, former governor of Massachusetts and an '08 presidential candidate, came to national prominence on the basis of a statewide health plan that he and the Massachusetts Legislature cooked up.

20. Germany's system is not single payer, in that they still have a quasi-private insurance industry. It is, however, heavily regulated and nonprofit, with the pricing structure largely set by the government.

21. Ezra Klein, "The Health of Nations," *American Prospect*, May 2007, p. 18.

22. Philip Mattera, "Saving Private Insurance: The Dubious Mission of Healthcare Reform," *Corporate Research Project*, E-Letter No. 63, January–February 2007, http://www.corp-research.org/archives/jan-feb07.htm. This memo details the magnitude and profits of the health insurance industry. UnitedHealth and WellPoint, the two largest for-profit health insurers, had joint 2006 revenues of about $155 billion; the combined profits of the top six insurance companies that year totaled $10 billion.

Sociologist Donald Light points out, "Profit margins of the major pharmaceutical companies have been consistently two to four times greater than the average for Fortune 500 companies, an indication of excess profits . . . ." ("Misleading Congress about Drug Development," *Journal of Health Politics, Policy and Law*, 32[5], 2007.)

23. Though let's not carry this explanation too far: Recent wage trends for persons without employer-provided health care have not outpaced those who get health care through the job. See Economic Policy Institute, "Economic Snapshot for April 12, 2006," http://www.epi.org/content.cfm/webfeatures _snapshots_20060412.

24. See Ezra Klein, "Cost Counts," *American Prospect*, April 12, 2007, Tapped, http://www.prospect.org/cs/articles?article=cost_counts.

25. Ibid.

26. CBO Testimony, Statement of Peter R. Orszag, Director, "Health Care and the Budget: Issues and Challenges for Reform," Congressional Budget Office, June 21, 2007, http://www.cbo.gov/ftpdocs/82xx/doc8255/06-21-HealthCareReform.pdf.

27. The quality-of-care measure is based on Medicare beneficiaries in the fee-for-service program who were hospitalized in 2004. It is the percentage who received recommended care for myocardial infarction, heart failure, and pneumonia.

28. See Merrill Goozner's blog, GoozNews, http://www.gooznews.com/.

29. Merrill Goozner, in "Healthy Bottom Lines," *American Prospect*, February 21, 2007, http://www.prospect.org/web/page.ww?section=root&name =ViewWeb&articleId=12399#goozner.

30. Atul Gawande, "Can This Patient Be Saved?" *New York Times*, May 5, 2007, http://query.nytimes.com/gst/fullpage.html?res=9C02E6D8113EF936A35756C 0A9619C8B63.

31. Source: U.S. Bureau of the Census, http://www.census.gov/hhes/www /poverty/histpov/hstpov2.html.

32. The original measure was devised in the early 1960s by Mollie Orshansky, who worked for the Social Security Administration. In 2001, in response to complaints about the validity of the measure, Orshansky told an interviewer, "Anyone who thinks we ought to change it is perfectly right."

33. Income in the official measure includes any cash provided by the government, like welfare benefits, but doesn't account for taxes and a lot of other stuff, as discussed in the text.

34. See U.S. Department of Health and Human Services, *Family Food Plans and Food Costs*, November 1962, p. 25, http://aspe.hhs.gov/poverty /familyfoodplan.pdf.

35. Bureau of Labor Statistics, "At Issue: Tracking Changes in Consumers' Spending Habits," *Monthly Labor Review*, September 1999.

36. Adam Smith, *Wealth of Nations*, 1776. For context, see *An Inquiry into the Nature and Causes of the Wealth of Nations*, Book Five, Chapter II, http://www .adamsmith.org/smith/won/won-b5-c2-article-4-ss2.html. John Cassidy provides this quote in his *New Yorker* article "Relatively Deprived," April 3, 2006, http://www.newyorker.com/printables /fact/060403fa_fact.

37. W. Michael Cox and Richard Alm, as quoted by Cassidy, ibid.

38. Doug Besharov, "Poor America," *Wall Street Journal*, March 24, 2006.

39. U.S. Census Bureau, Poverty Measurement Studies and Alternative Measures, "Tables of Alternative Poverty Estimates: 2005," http://www .census.gov/hhes/www/povmeas/tables.html. In fact, they give us 12 alternatives from which to choose. I consider this one—CMB-GA-CE—the most accurate, but please don't ask me to explain why (it gets the closest to solving the problems mentioned in the text). The average of all the alternatives runs about a percentage point above the official rate.

40. Unfortunately, we're stuck with the official measure, which has a particularly big shortcoming for this argument: It doesn't add the value of the Earned Income Credit, the wage subsidy for low-income workers that was significantly expanded in the early 1990s. Its inclusion would show an even larger downward trend.

41. In economic terms, poverty policy has become somewhat too "pro-cyclical" as opposed to "counter-cyclical." It helps lower poverty when the cycle is booming but doesn't catch enough people in the safety net when we're in recession.

42. Real median weekly earnings are for full-time workers, Bureau of Labor Statistics, http://www.bls.gov/cps/cpswktabs.htm, series No. LEU0252881600.

43. See this study by Sylvia A. Allegretto, Sean P. Corcoran, and Lawrence Mishel, "How Does Teacher Pay Compare? Methodological Challenges and Answers," Economic Policy Institute, August 2004, http://www.epinet.org /content.cfm/books_teacher_pay#intro, which finds, "Several types of analyses show that teachers earn significantly less than comparable workers, and this wage disadvantage has grown considerably over the last 10 years."

44. See Economic Policy Institute, Economic Snapshots, "Low Income Hinders College Attendance for Even the Highest Achieving Students," October 12, 2005, http://www.epi.org/content.cfm/webfeatures_snapshots_20051012.

45. Richard B. Freeman and Alexander Gelber, "Optimal Inequality/Optimal Incentives: Evidence from a Tournament," Social Science Research Network, October 2006, http://papers.ssrn.com/sol3/papers.cfm?abstract _id=936589.

46. Gary S. Becker and Kevin M. Murphy, "The Upside of Income Inequality," *The American*, May/June 2007, http://www.american.com/archive/2007 /may-june-magazine-contents/the-upside-of-income-inequality.

47. This finding is from an unpublished presentation given by Gary Burtless, Brookings Institution, based on OECD data. Burtless shows larger gains in tertiary education in most other countries, relative to the U.S., over the past decade. Some of this is "catch-up" but some countries—Canada, Japan, Sweden, Finland, Norway, Belgium—have surpassed the U.S. in terms of share with tertiary attainment (equivalent to our college degrees).

48. This statistic is for 18- to 64-year-olds in 2006.

49. U.S. Department of Labor, Bureau of Labor Statistics, Employment Projections, "Table 3. Occupations with the largest job growth, 2004–14," http://www.bls.gov/emp/mlrtab3.pdf.

50. In research I did with Larry Mishel and James Lin, we found that about a third of jobs vulnerable to offshoring (based on job characteristics that would facilitate the work being done elsewhere, like the lack of dependence on face time with clients) were jobs held by college-educated workers, including 10 percent with a masters degree or higher. See "The Characteristics of Offshorable Jobs," at http://www.epi.org/content.cfm /webfeatures_viewpoints_characteristics_of_offshorable_jobs.

51. Eduardo Porter, "More Than Ever, It Pays to Be the Top Executive," *New York Times*, May 25, 2007, http://query.nytimes.com/gst/fullpage.html ?res =9B03EED71630F936A15756C0A9619C8B63.

52. Thomas Piketty and Emmanuel Saez, "Income Inequality in the United States, 1913–1998 (updated to 2005), http://elsa.berkeley.edu/~saez/.

53. Ibid.

54. The comment was made by Randal Quarles, undersecretary of the Treasury. Quoted in Jonathan Weisman, "Snow Concedes Economic Surge Is Not Benefiting People Equally," *Washington Post*, August 9, 2005.

CHAPTER 2: DON'T KNOW MUCH ABOUT GDP

1. I'm now totally loaded for this triple-double reference to come up in conversation. It's when a player posts double digits in three categories, like points, assists, and rebounds.

2. Peruse the Web site of Redefining Progress (http://www.rprogress.org /index.htm) for state-of-the-art work in this area.

3. There were about 400,000 discouraged workers in 2006, and many more— just under five million—who said that, while they were out of the job market, they were available for work if something came up.

4. OK, I'm about to hit you with what has to be the most trivial bit of economics knowledge you've ever heard. When the first Friday of the month falls on the first day of the month, and the prior month has fewer than 31 days, the jobs report comes out on the second Friday. I can't say where, I can't say when, but someday you're going to pull that fact out of the air and blow your friends away—of course, there's also the risk that instead of blowing them away, you will *drive* them away.

5. For a detailed discussion of Friedman's theory, which did at one time— 30 years ago—fit the data, see Jared Bernstein, "Monetary Policy and the State of the Economy," Testimony Before the Committee on Financial Services, U.S. House of Representatives, February 16, 2007, http://www .house.gov/apps/list/hearing/financialsvcs_dem/htbernstein021607.pdf.

6. According to Rebecca Blank and Alan Blinder (1985), statistical analysis of these relationships reveals that "unemployment has very large and negative effects on the poor, while inflation appears to have few effects at all." See their paper, *Macroeconomics, Income Distribution, and Poverty*, NBER Working Paper Series, vol. w1567, Social Science Research Network, http://papers.ssrn.com/sol3/papers.cfm?abstract_id=268184.

7. See Jared Bernstein and Dean Baker, *The Benefits of Full Employment: When Markets Work for People* (Economic Policy Institute, 2003), http://www .epi.org/content.cfm/books_full_employment.

8. The underemployment rate (my term, not theirs) is from Table A-12 in the monthly employment report from the Bureau of Labor Statistics, definition U-6 (http://www.bls.gov/webapps/legacy/cpsatab12.htm).

9. See Daniel E. Hecker, "Reconciling Conflicting Data on Jobs for College Graduates," *Monthly Labor Review Online*, July 1992, http://www.bls .gov/opub/mlr/1992/07/art1abs.htm.

10. In a yet-to-be-published work, I've used the highly detailed job descriptions from the relatively new BLS National Compensation Survey to evaluate the extent of underutilized college-educated workers, and come up with about 15 percent in the 2000s, implying about six million such workers.

11. In the first example here—the new doughnut machine—productivity would rise as I describe, but "total factor productivity," which accounts for not only labor inputs but also capital inputs, might not. In the other examples, both types of productivity would rise, because we'd be making more doughnuts without new machines.

12. The White House, "At O'Hare, President Says 'Get on Board,'" September 27, 2001, http://www.whitehouse.gov/news/releases/2001/09/20010927-1 .html.

13. Technically, productivity is expected to rise with average compensation, not median family income, but it used to feed into family income and is much less likely to do so now for the reasons discussed in the text. In fact, in recent years, productivity growth has diverged from average compensation as well.

14. Just so you know I'm not making this stuff up, here is a pretty clear description of this process by no less than Big Ben Bernanke, chairman of the Federal Reserve: "I use the term 'anchored' to mean relatively insensitive to incoming data. So, for example, if the public experiences a spell of inflation higher than their long-run expectation, but their long-run expectation of inflation changes little as a result, then inflation expectations are well anchored. If, on the other hand, the public reacts to a short period of higher-than-expected inflation by marking up their long-run expectation considerably, then expectations are poorly anchored" (Ben S. Bernanke,

"Inflation Expectations and Inflation Forecasting" [speech, Monetary Economics Workshop of the National Bureau of Economic Research Summer Institute, Cambridge, Massachusetts, July 10, 2007], http://www.federalreserve.gov/boarddocs/speeches/2007/20070710/default.htm). The goal from the Fed's perspective is to have inflation well anchored at low levels, around 2 percent per year for "core" inflation (price growth excluding more volatile food and energy prices).

15. For example, if you owe someone money, inflation can help you and hurt them, because you're paying them back in less valuable dollars. Inflation, or, more precisely, greater inflation than was expected, reduces the real amount of the loan. So debtors tend to do better than creditors under a higher-inflation scenario.

16. Business Cycle Dating Committee, National Bureau of Economic Research, "The NBER's Recession Dating Procedure," October 21, 2003, http://www.nber.org/cycles/recessions.html.

17. Energy consumption per dollar of GDP has fallen by half over the last 50 years (Energy Information Administration, Annual Energy Review, "Table 1.5, Energy Consumption, Expenditures, and Emissions Indicators, 1949–2006," posted June 27, 2007, http://www.eia.doe.gov/emeu/aer/txt/ptb0105.html).

18. See Stacey L. Schreft and Aarti Singh, "A Closer Look at Jobless Recoveries," Economic Review, 2003, Federal Reserve Bank of Kansas City, http://www.kansascityfed.org/PUBLICAT/ECONREV/PDF/2q03schr.pdf.

19. Check out the cool organization WashTech, a unionlike group created to help boost the bargaining power of tech workers such as the Microsoft "permatemps" (http://www.washtech.org).

20. This is from my analysis of Bureau of Labor Statistics data on employment and involuntary part-time work ("part-time for economic reasons"). I compare the share of involuntary part-timers in the first month of an expansion with the share in the same month two years later. Any of you wonkish enough to try this at home will observe a large drop in the level of part-timers post-1994. This is due to a change in the wording of the survey question used by the BLS to measure this stuff.

21. Alan Greenspan, "Economic Volatility" (speech at a symposium sponsored by the Federal Reserve Bank of Kansas City, Jackson Hole, Wyoming,

August 30, 2002), http://www.federalreserve.gov/boarddocs/speeches /2002/20020830/.

22. Basically, we don't want people to take on clearly unaffordable loans, but recent developments in financial markets encourage this behavior. Specifically, lending institutions now often originate loans but no longer hold them (they sell them to other entities). This process undermines the market discipline that served in the past to make lenders more cautious— that is, it reduced the incentive to be careful about whom they made the loans to.

23. For example, the 1979 edition of Alan Blinder's much used textbook, *Economics: Principles and Policy*, told students: "[T]he minimum wage effectively bans the employment of workers whose marginal product is less than [the minimum wage]. The primary consequence of the minimum wage law is not an increase in the incomes of the least skilled workers but a restriction of their employment opportunities" (p. 519).

   The book's tenth edition (2006), however, framed the issue this way: "Elementary economic reasoning . . . suggests that setting a minimum wage . . . above the free-market wage . . . must cause unemployment. . . . Indeed, earlier editions of this book, for example, confidently told students that a higher minimum wage must lead to higher unemployment. But some surprising economic research published in the 1990s cast serious doubt on this conventional wisdom" (p. 493).

24. See http://www.livingwagecampaign.org/index.php?id=1959 for a list of cities with living wage ordinances. The list is compiled by the community activist group ACORN. They've had great success in this area.

25. See Jared Bernstein, "The Living Wage Movement: What Is It, Why Is It, and What's Known about Its Impact?" in Richard B. Freeman, Joni Hersch, and Lawrence Mishel, eds., *Emerging Labor Market Institutions for the Twenty-First Century*, National Bureau of Economic Research Conference Report (Chicago: University of Chicago Press, 2004).

26. Poverty expert Nancy K. Cauthen wrote a very useful and readable paper in favor of work supports: *Improving Work Supports*, 2007, Economic Policy Institute, http://www.sharedprosperity.org/bp198.html.

27. Some of the best work on the productivity/efficiency impacts of higher minimum wages comes from the Berkeley University researchers Arin

Dube and Michael Reich (along with other coauthors). For those who want to dig deeper, examine their compelling work at "Minimum Wage Research," Institute for Research on Labor and Employment, http://www.irle.berkeley.edu/research/minimumwage.html.

CHAPTER 3: POLITICAL ECONOMY 202

1. *All Together Now: Common Sense for a Fair Economy* (San Francisco: Berrett-Koehler Publishers, 2006).

2. Hillary Clinton, "Economic Policy: Modern Progressive Vision: Shared Prosperity" (speech, May 29, 2007), http://www.hillaryclinton.com /news/speech/view/?id=1839.

3. MetLife, *The MetLife Study of the American Dream: Against the Backdrop of the Financial Burden Shift*, January 25, 2007, p. 7, http://www.metlife.com /WPSAssets/23720648601169583027V1FMetLifeAmericanDreamStudyFinal 012507.pdf. Gen Xers are defined as those born between 1965 and 1976.

4. Social Security was introduced in the mid-1930s; there are also disability and surviving spouse components, but we'll stick with the most significant part: retiree pensions.

5. We also leave behind more pollution, but we'll talk about that later.

6. U.S. Social Security Administration, Office of the Chief Actuary, *The 2007 OASDI Trustees Report*, "V. Assumptions and Methods Underlying Actuarial Estimates, B. Economic Assumptions and Methods," updated April 23, 2007, http://www.ssa.gov/OACT/TR/TR07/V_economic.html.

7. Chad Stone and Robert Greenstein, "What the 2007 Trustees' Report Shows About Social Security," Table 2, Center on Budget and Policy Priorities, April 24, 2007, http://www.cbpp.org/4-24-07socsec.pdf.

8. L. Josh Bivens, *Social Security's Fixable Financing Issues: Shortfall in Funds Is Not Inevitable*, Economic Policy Institute, April 26, 2005, http://www.epinet.org /content.cfm/ib207.

9. Economist Ed Wolff estimates that of those households nearing retirement, the share that will be unable to replace at least half of their preretirement income rose from about 30 percent in the late 1980s to about 42 percent in the late 1990s. For minority households, who, by the way,

benefit disproportionately from Social Security, that share was 53 percent (Edward N. Wolff, "Retirement Insecurity: The Income Shortfalls Awaiting the Soon-to-Retire," Economic Policy Institute, May 2002, http://www.epi .org/content.cfm/books_retirement_intro).

10. See Alicia H. Munnell and Steven A. Sass, "Social Security and the Stock Market: Lessons from Around the World," *Employment Research*, Upjohn Institute, January 2007, http://www.upjohninst.org/publications /newsletter/AHM-SAS_107.pdf.

11. Actually, the timing question regarding economic stimulus has become more complicated in recent years. As we discussed in the recession section, the last few official downturns were relatively mild in terms of real GDP contraction, but long and deep regarding job loss. After the 2001 recession, for example, the unemployment rate kept rising for 15 months! Thus, a stimulus package that might be considered late when targeting GDP could be timely as far as unemployment is concerned. If you want to read more about this see the blog post I wrote with Larry Mishel: http://www.tpmcafe .com/blog/coffeehouse/2008/jan/15/better_late_than_never.

12. Citizens for Tax Justice, *The Bush Tax Cuts: The Latest CTJ Data*, March 2007, http://www.ctj.org/pdf/gwbdata.pdf.

13. Paul Krugman wrote a piece about Bush's actions in this mode called "Dooh Nibor Economics," http://query.nytimes.com/gst/fullpage .html?res=9B04E2DB1631F932A35755C0A9629C8B63.

14. As noted in the text, a similar dynamic occurred in 2007, as investors slowly became aware that the asset packages they were holding contained some very shaky mortgage debt. As those debts defaulted, credit markets froze, and the economy hit the skids. The Fed actively intervened in ways that, as of this writing in early 2008, have had modestly warming effects on the chilled credit market.

15. This point was made to me by my good, old friend James "Doc" Halliday, who knows more than a little about company balance sheets.

16. See transcript, the Agenda for Shared Prosperity, April 12, 2007, http://www.sharedprosperity.org/av/070412/20070412-transcript-stiglitz .pdf.

17. Source: Bureau of Economic Analysis, National Income and Product Accounts (http://www.bea.gov/bea/dn/nipaweb/index.asp).

18. Korb is a defense analyst at the Center for American Progress. See this document, from the Congressional Progressive Caucus, for more on his input to this debate: *Fiscal Year 2008–17 "Peace & Security" Budget Alternative*, http://www.tompaine.com/docs/Inspiration_Budget_Illustrative_Text.htm.

19. Ibid.

20. This article has the relevant links: Jared Bernstein and Deborah Weinstein, "The Inspiration Budget," TomPaine.com, April 2, 2007, http://www.tompaine.com/articles/2007/04/02/the_inspiration_budget.php.

21. Chris L. Jenkins, "Long Wait List for Va. Child-Care Subsidy Pushes Parents to Choose Lesser of Evils," *Washington Post*, March 6, 2007, http://www.washingtonpost.com/wp-dyn/content/article/2007/03/05/AR2007030501626.html.

22. CBO Testimony, Statement of Robert A. Sunshine, Assistant Director for Budget Analysis, "Estimated Costs of U.S. Operations in Iraq and Afghanistan and of Other Activities Related to the War on Terrorism," Congressional Budget Office, July 31, 2007, http://www.cbo.gov/ftpdocs/84xx/doc8497/07-30-WarCosts_Testimony.pdf.

23. Jared Bernstein, "Tax Incentives for Businesses in Response to a Minimum Wage Increase (testimony before the U.S. Senate Committee on Finance, January 10, 2007), Economic Policy Institute, http://www.epi.org/content.cfm/webfeatures_viewpoints_minwage_tax_incentives_testimony_01102007.

24. Lawrence Mishel (testimony before the Labor-HHS Education Subcommittee, Appropriations Committee, U.S. House of Representatives, February 15, 2007), Economic Policy Institute, http://www.epi.org/content.cfm/webfeatures_viewpoints_living_standards_and_ed_testimony.

25. See CBO Testimony, Statement of Robert A. Sunshine, "Estimated Costs of U.S. Operations in Iraq and Afghanistan," July 31, 2007, p. 1, http://www.cbo.gov/ftpdocs/84xx/doc8497/07-30-WarCosts_Testimony.pdf.

26. Robert J. Samuelson, "A $2 Trillion Footnote?" *Washington Post*, February 28, 2007, http://www.washingtonpost.com/wp-dyn/content/article/2007/02/27/AR2007022701159.html.

27. Erik Eckholm, "Plight Deepens for Black Men, Studies Warn," *New York Times*, March 20, 2006, http://www.nytimes.com/2006/03/20/national/20blackmen.html?ei=5090&en=57e0d1ceebcbc209&ex=1300510800&pagewanted=print.

28. Steve Savner and Jared Bernstein, "Can Better Skills Meet Better Jobs?" *American Prospect*, August 13, 2004, http://www.prospect.org/cs/articles?articleId=8357.

29. He's the lawyer on the TV show *Boston Legal* who always gets assigned impossible cases like this.

CHAPTER 4: THE WORLD AIN'T FLAT AS ALL THAT

1. Sounds ridiculously obvious, but it's not. Country A makes both widgets and wine more efficiently than country B. But country B makes wine more efficiently than it makes widgets. Comparative advantage teaches us that both countries will end up better off if A specializes in widgets and B in wine (and of course, they sell them to each other). This holds even though A makes wine more efficiently than does B. Maybe a more obvious example is the lawyer who types faster than her secretary. The two of them will be more productive if the lawyer sticks to law and the secretary does the typing. Trade makes countries better off when they specialize in producing those things in which they have a comparative, not an absolute, advantage.

2. Eric Alterman, "Dude! Where's My Debate?" *The Nation*, February 26, 2007, http://www.thenation.com/doc/20070226/alterman.

3. China joined the World Trade Organization in 1999, but that's not a "trade deal." Also, research has found little relationship between Chinese penetration of our markets and WTO status (Andrew K. Rose, "Do We Really Know That the WTO Increases Trade?" [draft, October 3, 2003, forthcoming: *American Economic Review*], University of California, Berkeley, Haas School of Business, http://faculty.haas.berkeley.edu/arose/GATTshort.pdf).

4. See Josh Bivens, "Globalization, American Wages, and Inequality: Past, Present, and Future," http://www.epi.org/workingpapers/wp279.pdf.

5. See Bivens, "Globalization and American Wages: Today and Tomorrow," http://www.epi.org/content.cfm/bp196.

6. Josh Bivens, "Cutting to the Chase," TPM Cafe, February 28, 2007, http://www.tpmcafe.com/blog/specialguests/2007/feb/28/cutting_to_the_chase.

7. That is, we're more productive—we add more value in an hour of work than they do—so their productivity growth rate is faster than ours. It's not unusual for developing countries to have relatively fast rates of productivity growth, largely because they're starting from very low levels. For evi-

dence regarding Chinese productivity growth, see Zuliu Hu and Mohsin S. Khan, "Why Is China Growing So Fast?" International Monetary Fund, http://www.imf.org/external/pubs/ft/issues8/index.htm#Boom.

8. See Jeff Faux's book *The Global Class War* (Hoboken, New Jersey: John Wiley & Sons, 2006) on these points.

9. See John Schmitt, *The Rise in Job Displacement, 1991–2004: The Crisis in American Manufacturing*, Center for Economic and Policy Research, August 2004, http://www.cepr.net/documents/publications/labor_markets_2004_08.pdf.

10. See note 1 above for a discussion of *comparative advantage*, the theory behind this outcome. If we're talking about cheap manufactured goods like textiles, developing countries with lots of cheap labor have a comparative advantage that makes this a good deal for both parties, according to the theory.

11. The poll, by Lake Research Partners, is here: http://www.changetowin .org/fileadmin/pdf/topline.CTW.Workers.R.040307.pdf. The full question is: "Looking to the next generation, the way things are going now, do you feel the American Dream will be easier to reach than today, harder to reach, or will it be the same?"

12. David Leonhardt, "Looking for the Angry Populists in Suburbia," *New York Times*, January 28, 2007, http://www.nytimes.com/2007/01/28/weekinreview /28leon.html?_r=1&oref=slogin.

13. Pew Research Center, *Once Again, the Future Ain't What It Used to Be*, May 2, 2006, http://pewresearch.org/assets/social/pdf/BetterOff.pdf.

14. *New York Times*/CBS News Poll, February 23–27, 2007, http://graphics8 .nytimes.com/packages/pdf/national/03022007_poll.pdf

15. Some of this material was written jointly with Josh Bivens and posted on various blogs, including the Huffington Post and TPM Cafe.

16. Ylan Q. Mui, "Circuit City Cuts 3,400 'Overpaid' Workers," *Washington Post*, March 29, 2007, http://www.washingtonpost.com/wp-dyn/content/article /2007/03/28/AR2007032802185.html.

17. What's the "40th percentile wage"? Forty percent of the workforce earns less than this wage; 60 percent earns more.

18. Pew Research Center for the People & the Press, *Trends in Political Values and Core Attitudes: 1987–2007*, March 22, 2007, p. 27, http://people-press.org /reports/pdf/312.pdf.

19. See George Borjas and and Lawrence Katz, *The Evolution of the Mexican Born Workforce in the United States*, NBER Working Paper #11281, 2005, Tbl 11, http://www.nber.org/papers/w11281.

20. Ray Marshall, *Getting Immigration Reform Right*, EPI Briefing Paper, Economic Policy Institute, March 15, 2007, http://www.sharedprosperity.org/bp186 /bp186.pdf.

21. Jeff Faux, "South of the Border: The Impact of Mexico's Economic Woes," *San Francisco Chronicle*, May 18, 2006.

22. Robert Pear, "After Aiding Bill on Immigration, Employers Balk," *New York Times*, May 21, 2007, http://query.nytimes.com/gst/fullpage.html?res =9B02E4D61E31F932A15756C0A9619C8B63.

23. See Dean Baker, "The Conservative Nanny State: How the Wealthy Use the Government to Stay Rich and Get Richer," Center for Economic and Policy Research, http://www.conservativenannystate.org.

24. Jared Bernstein, L. Josh Bivens, and Arindrajit Dube, *Wrestling with Wal-mart: Tradeoffs Between Profits, Prices, and Wages*, EPI Working Paper, Economic Policy Institute, June 15, 2006, http://www.epinet.org/workingpapers/wp276.pdf.

25. As a share of GDP, unbalanced trade with China accounts for 41 percent of the increase in the trade deficit since 2001.

26. The British economist Nicholas Stern did the most comprehensive study on the costs of ignoring global warming and found them to be potentially staggering, analogous to those of a major recession if not depression. Critics argued that Stern's loss estimates were too high because he overestimated the extent of damage from climate change, and he did not discount the future at all (arguing, in essence, that a dollar saved today is worth an inflation-adjusted dollar many years hence; that's not very realistic, since a dollar invested today should return much more than a dollar many years from now). That may be an extreme assumption, but as I suggest in the text, economists are likely to over-discount the future in this debate.

27. See Associated Press, "Smithsonian Alters Climate Exhibition," *New York Times*, May 22, 2007, http://www.nytimes.com/2007/05/22/washington /22brfs-SMITHSONIANA_BRF.html?ei=5070&en=95bfdfad82bc0cec&ex =1181620800&adxnnl=1&adxnnlx=1181505930-4DkaTLPduHFj+LSRefjJsg.

28. You can have a positive externality, too, where someone doesn't get paid for the benefits of his actions. If I'm your neighbor and I have a beautiful

garden that you see, smell, and enjoy, yet you pay nothing for such pleasures, I'm generating a positive externality.

29. Yes, they're still working out the system. Most countries started by experimenting with *cap and trade* systems, where polluters are allotted a certain amount of emissions credits. If they use less than their allotted amount, they can sell the rest. This is proving to be less efficient than more direct methods of taxation, which some countries are moving toward.

30. John M. Broder and Andrew C. Revkin, "Warming Is Seen as Wiping Out Most Polar Bears," *New York Times*, September 8, 2007, http://www.nytimes .com/2007/09/08/science/earth/08polar.html.

CHAPTER 5: THE RECONNECTION AGENDA

1. U.S. Representative Barney Frank (D-Massachusetts) gets this connection, and upon his ascension to chair of the House Financial Services Committee in 2006, he began holding hearings on the issue (House Committee on Financial Services, Full Committee Hearing, "The State of the Economy, the State of the Labor Market, and the Conduct of Monetary Policy," February 16, 2007, http://www.house.gov/apps/list/hearing/financialsvcs _dem/ht021607.shtml).

2. While full employment is usually discussed in terms of low unemployment, a better measure these days is the rate of employment—the share of the working-age population with jobs. That's remained low in the 2000s, in part due to an underappreciated problem in this cycle: the lack of robust job creation. In fact, as of this writing (mid-2007), one BLS survey shows that the rate of job creation is the lowest on record, going back to the early 1990s (see "gross job gains as a percent of employment" in Table 2 here for the third quarter 2006: U.S. Department of Labor, Bureau of Labor Statistics, *Business Employment Dynamics: Fourth Quarter 2006*, August 16, 2007, http://www.bls.gov/news.release/pdf/cewbd.pdf).

3. See Steve Savner and Jared Bernstein, "Can Better Skills Meet Better Jobs?" *American Prospect*, August 13, 2004, http://www.prospect.org/cs/articles ?article=can_better_skills_meet_better_jobs.

4. Of course, deep-pocketed union busters have opposed EFCA (the Employee Free Choice Act) forever and always will. But for many objective folks, the act has foundered due to one provision: It offers an alternative to

secret ballots, called "card check"—if enough workers in a bargaining unit sign cards, management must recognize the union. Many folks abhor this aspect of the bill because they feel any idea that precludes secret balloting is suspect.

So here's my idea. One reason the secret ballot process often fails in potential union settings is that it takes weeks and months for the election to take place. This gives employers, who hold all the cards—union organizers aren't allowed on the site, while management can hold all the anti-union meetings it wants—time to make it clear to the workforce that they support the union at great risk to their livelihoods.

The solution is to make it the law of the land that the vote take place, by secret ballot, within days, preferably one or two, of the request to form the union. This cuts off management's ability to run an extensive anti-union propaganda campaign and preserves the secret ballot.

5. See Lawrence Mishel, Jared Bernstein, and Sylvia Allegretto, *The State of Working America 2006/2007*, Economic Policy Institute, Table 3.38, http://www.stateofworkingamerica.org/tabfig/03/SWA06_Table3.38.jpg. The union advantage for workers in the bottom fifth is 2.7 times that of workers in the top fifth of the wage scale.

6. For a good example of Mahar's work in this area, see "The State of the Nation's Health," *Dartmouth Medicine*, Spring 2007, http://dartmed.dartmouth.edu/spring07/html/atlas.php.

7. Joseph E. Stiglitz, "Prizes, Not Patents," *Project Syndicate*, http://www.project-syndicate.org/commentary/stiglitz81.

8. Political scientist Jacob Hacker has a very thoughtful plan in this spirit (full disclosure: My organization, the Economic Policy Institute, has promoted this plan, but it's not like we're getting any $ to do so! We just really like it). See Jacob S. Hacker, *Health Care for America*, Economic Policy Institute, January 11, 2007, http://www.sharedprosperity.org/bp180.html.

9. Though he doesn't like to talk about it, Republican presidential candidate Mitt Romney crafted a health care plan in Massachusetts in the spirit of the above discussion, as did Republican Governor Arnold Schwarzenegger of California. Both plans stress universal coverage through individual mandates (you've got to be covered; without this requirement, it's tougher to control costs due to adverse selection; also, there's not much chance of success in zeroing out the "uninsurance rate"). Both plans also are a bit

skimpy in important ways. The subsidies are too small, so you're telling folks to get covered but not offering them enough help to close the deal. Also, the taxes they charge businesses to pay for expanded public coverage look too low. But they both represent good starts. Like Bill Clinton used to say in a gravelly voice while pointing a knuckle at us: "Don't let the best be the enemy of the good."

10. A May 2007 *New York Times*/CBS poll, for example, asked whether respondents supported the path to citizenship and guest worker provisions in the Senate immigration reform bill. In both cases, two-thirds of respondents did so (http://www.nytimes.com/2007/05/25/us/25poll.html?_r=1&oref =slogin). An ABC News/*Washington Post* poll from late 2006 found that 60 percent of respondents said that "undocumented workers should be given the opportunity to stay and become citizens" (http://www.washingtonpost.com /wp-dyn/content/article/2006/01/02/AR2006010201376.html).

11. See Richard Rothstein, *Class and Schools: Using Social, Economic, and Educational Reform to Close the Black-White Achievement Gap*, Economic Policy Institute, 2004, http://www.epinet.org/content.cfm/books_class_and_schools.

12. The Rothstein book cited above discusses this literature in some detail.

13. Here's the graph, "Figure 2F, College completion by income status and test scores," from our book *State of Working America* . . . view it and weep: http://www.stateofworkingamerica.org/tabfig/02/SWA06_Fig2F.jpg.

14. See Martin Carnoy et al., *The Charter School Dust-Up: Examining the Evidence on Enrollment and Achievement*, Economic Policy Institute, http://www.epinet .org/content.cfm/book_charter_school.

15. See Apollo Alliance, http://www.apolloalliance.org/.

16. See this op-ed I wrote with a colleague, the tireless poverty warrior Mark Greenberg: "A Plan to End Child Poverty," *Washington Post*, April 3, 2006, http://www.washingtonpost.com/wp-dyn/content/article/2006/04/02 /AR2006040201091.html.

17. The 2008 presidential candidate John Edwards signed on to this idea, touting a target to eliminate poverty in 30 years and an elaborate plan to reconnect poverty reduction to economic growth.

1. The best evidence for this claim is the right-track/wrong-track questions regarding the direction in which the country is headed. Numerous polls track these same questions, and in mid-2007, the *Newsweek*, Harris, NBC News/*Wall Street Journal*, L.A. *Times*/Bloomberg, N.Y. *Times*/CBS, and AP/Ipsos polls all registered disapproval at or near historic highs, with around 70 percent of respondents saying the country was on the wrong track.

Acknowledgments

It took a village to raise this book. At the heart of the book are real people's questions about the economy. I collected many of these questions myself, but I also got a lot of help from the staff of Berrett-Koehler. Questioners included Bob Liss, Ian Bach, Ken Lupoff, Maria Jesus Aguilo, Julia Charles, Ann Matranga, Doug from California, David from Illinois, Chuck from California, and the scores of others who submitted questions via e-mail and blog comments. I owe many thanks to these curious readers, who were kind enough to devote some time to thinking up and submitting interesting stumpers for me to tackle.

As with my previous book for Berrett-Koehler, my editor, Johanna Vondeling, was a great source of encouragement, inspiration, and guidance. Her ear for what works and what doesn't continues to be an invaluable resource. She's one of those rare people who can zero in on minutiae while never losing sight of the big picture. I also want to thank Steve Piersanti and Jeevan Sivasubramaniam for their support and encouragement. Elissa Rabellino and Kristi Hein provided careful, insightful, and enthusiastic copyediting.

My colleagues at the Economic Policy Institute never seem to get tired of educating me and providing me with a truly unique sounding board. I'm sure I'm biased, but I think they are the greatest collection of economists in one place on earth. Collaborations with my longtime friend and colleague Larry Mishel show up throughout the book; similarly, on international economics, I've incessantly consulted/bothered Josh Bivens, and on health care, Elise Gould. On politics, policy, and presentation, I've benefited from great discussions with Michael Ettlinger, David Kusnet, and Ross Eisenbrey. James Lin is a wonderfully careful, hardworking research assistant.

Between my family and that pesky day job, I experienced my own crunch finding the time I needed to write this book. I would never have done so but for the help of my wife, Kay Arndorfer, whose calm and patient support was and is always forthcoming. I also want to thank Ellie and Kate for avoiding the home office during writing times except when it was essential for me to see a handstand, magic trick, or some similarly urgent development.

Index

Index

Index

About the Author

Jared Bernstein is a senior economist and director of the Living Standards Program at the Economic Policy Institute in Washington, DC. He is the author of the book *All Together Now: Common Sense for a Fair Economy* (Berrett-Koehler, 2006) and coauthored eight editions of *The State of Working America* (Economic Policy Institute). Bernstein is a frequent media commentator on economic matters and a contributor to CNBC. His commentary, blog postings, and op-eds appear in the *New York Times*, the *Washington Post*, and TPM Cafe.

Berrett-Koehler is an independent publisher dedicated to an ambitious mission: Creating a World that Works for All.

We believe that to truly create a better world, action is needed at all levels—individual, organizational, and societal. At the individual level, our publications help people align their lives and work with their deepest values. At the organizational level, our publications promote progressive leadership and management practices, socially responsible approaches to business, and humane and effective organizations. At the societal level, our publications advance social and economic justice, shared prosperity, sustainable development, and new solutions to national and global issues.

A major theme of our publications is "Opening Up New Space." They challenge conventional thinking, introduce new points of view, and offer new alternatives for change. Their common quest is changing the underlying beliefs, mindsets, institutions, and structures that keep generating the same cycles of problems, no matter who our leaders are or what improvement programs we adopt.

We strive to practice what we preach—to operate our publishing company in line with the ideas in our books. At the core of our approach is stewardship, which we define as a deep sense of responsibility to administer the company for the benefit of all of our "stakeholder" groups: authors, customers, employees, investors, service providers, and the communities and environment around us. We seek to establish a partnering relationship with each stakeholder that is open, equitable, and collaborative.

We are gratified that thousands of readers, authors, and other friends of the company consider themselves to be part of the "BK Community." We hope that you, too, will join our community and connect with us through the ways described on our website at www.bkconnection.com.

A BK CURRENTS TITLE

This book is part of our BK Currents series. BK Currents titles advance social and economic justice by exploring the critical intersections between business and society. Offering a unique combination of thoughtful analysis and progressive alternatives, BK Currents titles promote positive change at the national and global levels. To find out more, visit www.bkcurrents.com.

VISIT OUR WEBSITE

Go to www.bkconnection.com to read exclusive previews and excerpts of new books, find detailed information on all Berrett-Koehler titles and authors, browse subject-area libraries of books, and get special discounts.

SUBSCRIBE TO OUR FREE E-NEWSLETTER

Be the first to hear about new publications, special discount offers, exclusive articles, news about bestsellers, and more! Get on the list for our free e-newsletter by going to www.bkconnection.com.

PARTICIPATE IN THE DISCUSSION

To see what others are saying about our books and post your own thoughts, check out our blogs at www.bkblogs.com.

GET QUANTITY DISCOUNTS

Berrett-Koehler books are available at quantity discounts for orders of ten or more copies. Please call us toll-free at (800) 929-2929 or email us at bkp.orders@aidcvt.com.

HOST A READING GROUP

For tips on how to form and carry on a book reading group in your workplace or community, see our website at www.bkconnection.com.

JOIN THE BK COMMUNITY

Thousands of readers of our books have become part of the "BK Community" by participating in events featuring our authors, reviewing draft manuscripts of forthcoming books, spreading the word about their favorite books, and supporting our publishing program in other ways. If you would like to join the BK Community, please contact us at bkcommunity@bkpub.com.